The Rise

BOOKS BY PAUL SCHULLERY

Old Yellowstone Days (editor)

The Bears of Yellowstone

The Grand Canyon: Early Impressions (editor)

The Orvis Story (with Austin Hogan)

American Bears: Selections from the Writings of Theodore Roosevelt (editor)

Freshwater Wilderness: Yellowstone Fishes and Their World (with John D. Varley)

Mountain Time

Theodore Roosevelt: Wilderness Writings (editor)

The National Parks (editor and coauthor)

Wildlife in Transition: Man and Nature on Yellowstone's Northern Range
(with Don Despain, Douglas B. Houston, and Mary Meagher)

Island in the Sky: Pioneering Accounts of Mount Rainier (editor)

American Fly Fishing: A History

Bud Lilly's Guide to Western Fly Fishing (with Bud Lilly)

The Bear Hunter's Century: Profiles from the Golden Age of Bear Hunting

A Trout's Best Friend (with Bud Lilly)

Pregnant Bears and Crawdad Eyes: Excursions and Encounters in Animal Worlds

Yellowstone Bear Tales (editor)

The National Park Service: A Seventy-fifth Anniversary Album
(with William Sontag and Linda Griffin)

Yellowstone's Ski Pioneers: Peril and Heroism on the Winter Trail

Bears—Their Biology and Management
(proceedings, coedited with James Claar)

Glacier-Waterton: Land of Hanging Valleys

Shupton's Fancy: A Tale of the Fly-Fishing Obsession

Echoes from the Summit: Writings and Photographs (editor)

Mark of the Bear: Legend and Lore of an American Icon (editor)

The Yellowstone Wolf: A Guide and Sourcebook (editor)

Yellowstone's Northern Range: Complexity and Change in a Wildland Ecosystem
(with Norman A. Bishop, Francis J. Singer, and John D. Varley)

Searching for Yellowstone: Ecology and Wonder in the Last Wilderness

Royal Coachman: The Lore and Legends of Fly-Fishing

Bud Lilly's Guide to Fly Fishing the New West (with Bud Lilly)

*America's National Parks: The Spectacular Forces
That Shaped Our Treasured Lands*

Real Alaska: Finding Our Way in the Wild Country

Lewis and Clark among the Grizzlies: Legend and Legacy in the American West

Myth and History in the Creation of Yellowstone National Park
(with Lee H. Whittlesey)

People and Place: The Human Experience in Greater Yellowstone
(proceedings, coedited with Sarah Stevenson)

The Rise

Streamside Observations on Trout, Flies, and Fly Fishing

Paul Schullery

Photographs by the author

Illustrations by Marsha Karle

With additional illustrations from angling literature

STACKPOLE BOOKS

Published by
STACKPOLE BOOKS
5067 Ritter Road
Mechanicsburg, PA 17055
www.stackpolebooks.com

Printed in China

First edition

10 9 8 7 6 5 4 3 2 1

Library of Congress Cataloging-in-Publication Data

Schullery, Paul.
    The rise : streamside observations on trout, flies, and fly fishing /
  Paul Schullery ; photographs by the author ; illustrations by Marsha Karle ;
  with additional illustrations from angling literature.— 1st ed.
       p.   cm.
    Includes bibliographical references (p.   ) and index.
    ISBN-13: 978-0-8117-0182-2 (hardcover)
    ISBN-10: 0-8117-0182-4 (hardcover)
    1. Trout fishing.   2. Fly fishing.   I. Title.
SH687.S246   2006
799.17′57—dc22
                                                2005037913

For John Varley

If there is magic on this planet,
it is contained in water.

LOREN EISELEY, *The Immense Journey* (1957)

CONTENTS

Preface: Of New Things   xi

Part One: How Trout Take a Fly   1

   CHAPTER 1: *The River and the Bridge*   3

   CHAPTER 2: *The Take*   15

   CHAPTER 3: *Reading the Rise*   33

   CHAPTER 4: *Coping with Rejection*   63

   CHAPTER 5: *The Trout's Field of View*   77

   CHAPTER 6: *Are Trout Getting Smarter?*   89

Part Two: How We Take a Fly   103

   CHAPTER 7: *Tradition and Revolution*   105

   CHAPTER 8: *Deep Basics*   109

   CHAPTER 9: *Dogma and the Dry Fly*   117

   CHAPTER 10: *The Visible Hook*   125

   CHAPTER 11: *Hackles*   137

   CHAPTER 12: *Wings*   147

   CHAPTER 13: *Skippers, Skaters, Dappers, and Dancers*   159

   CHAPTER 14: *Antidotes to Madness*   175

Bibliography   179

Acknowledgments   185

Index   189

PREFACE:
OF NEW THINGS

The rise of a trout is far from being the only thing that matters about fly fishing, but it is for many of us the most exciting thing. As a thrilling act of predation and an exhilarating affirmation or devastating condemnation of our streamcraft, the rise is at the center of the small universe of interests, crafts, and passions that make up the sport. I'm far from the first to notice that all the other parts of fly fishing revolve, sometimes quite erratically and distantly, around that one crucial moment when a fish decides to feed.

It is both odd and wonderful that up until that instant, though we may have put immense amounts of time, thought, and energy into getting there, the trout has been without concern for us and our ways. The trout's wildness and independence are what make each cast so important to us.

In *A Sand County Almanac* (1949), the visionary ecologist-conservationist Aldo Leopold told of a brief "fishing idyl" on a Wisconsin trout stream. For a few minutes, he sat and considered "the ways of trout and men."

> How like fish we are: ready, nay eager, to seize upon whatever new thing some wind of circumstance shakes down upon the river of time. And how we rue our haste, finding the gilded morsel to contain a hook. Even so, I think there is some virtue in eagerness, whether its object prove true or false. How utterly dull would be a wholly prudent man, or trout, or world!

My fishing life, and I suspect those of many others, has been a testament to the sort of imprudence Leopold forgave and celebrated. I often arrive at the stream full of haste and eagerness, anxious for the first cast and the first sign of an imprudent trout. If a calmer pace is called for, I have to force upon myself the discipline of watchfulness. Unlike our famous angling masters, who have counseled extended sessions of careful observation, I'm likely to cast first and ask questions later. I'm just too energized for the stingily hoarded casts so eloquently recommended by Vincent Marinaro, and though I heed Walton's admonition to "study to be quiet," I rarely study to sit still.

Contradictorily, even while I'm so absorbed in finding the next cast, my attention may drift and scatter far beyond the stream's banks. I am taken with the serendipitously eventful quality of life along the stream, with things well removed from the catching of trout. Leopold's "new thing" is, for me, the relentless series of surprises and wonders I find in wild nature and moving water. There is too much to do here—too much to absorb, savor, and remember.

It has been said—and not only about fishing—that reading and thinking and talking about something are what we do when we are unable to do the thing itself. The point of this seems to be that such activities are mere consolation until the real thing is available again. That falls short of explaining how fishing works for me. The sport's sages tell us that the thoughtful angler is always studying and learning while fishing, but I seem to organize the whole business differently.

For me, fishing is when I soak up huge amounts of raw experience, renewed wonder, and unprocessed information, and not fishing is when I put my mind to work on that undifferentiated accumulation of impressions. When fishing occupies my nonfishing time, it isn't just a way of killing time until I can actually fish again. It's a way of catching up on all the parts of fishing I can't do when I'm too busy casting. This may not be the best way to go about the thing—certainly it would dismay the sport's role models—but it's involuntary anyway, so I go with it. It's when I study to be quiet.

And sometimes it works really well. It took the preoccupying mechanics of photography and an unfishable section of trout stream to finally make me look hard at how trout feed. And even then, I spent far less time on the stream getting the photographs than I have spent examining those pictures and comparing my impressions with those of the writers and scientists who had previously studied feeding trout—and the fly-fishing theorists who have tried to reason out what it was about a fly or technique that caused the trout to rise in the first place.

And it was only then, as I sorted through all this lore, history, and data, that I began to feel qualified to look back freshly on my own many years of experience with rising trout. The new thing will always be weighed and tested against all the old things.

* * *

I am pleased to admit that I am at heart a rather lazy fisherman and have never felt obliged to turn my entire fishing life into an empirical inquiry. In the urgency of arriving at the stream, I am as likely to start with a fly that I am fond of—or excited about because I just tied it—as a fly predicted to work by the prevailing hatch charts. I have fished a lot and for a long time, but nobody is going to take me for one of those hard-driving problem solvers—those admirable and athletic souls whose entire beings are engaged in perfecting fly patterns and presenting them flawlessly.

And yet I always have been enchanted by wild trout and our persistent, quixotic, and sometimes brilliant attempts to understand them well enough to catch them. There is nothing shallow about this enchantment. My approach to fly theory may be somewhat more reflective or even whimsical than those of the hard drivers, but luckily there are many ways to be serious about fishing.

We might casually think of the centuries of fly fishing that preceded us as rather like a long version of our own experiences, in which fly fishers have gradually become smarter and more proficient as the sport has aged. For many generations, the literature of fly fishing has been produced by people who obviously considered themselves substantially wiser than their predecessors. Though "progress" is as slippery a notion in fishing as it is in many other realms, sometimes those anglers may even have been right about their achievements.

But the comparison between the history of fly fishing and the career of a single fly fisher works another way. Just as most of what any generation of fly fishers knows has been passed down to them by their predecessors, so too do we individuals typically spend much, if not most, of our time learning—rediscovering, if you like—what has been learned countless times before.

Thus we build our sport's long tradition and our own fly-fishing wisdom in a happily complicated series of tiny increments, most of which don't take us in any clearly discernible direction, and some of which have nothing to do with the catching of fish. It's one big, gloriously sloppy experiment. There are indeed those discoveries that we like to think of as progress, but there are also false starts, embarrassments, and dead ends galore. That most of what we learn is not new does not lessen the personal excitement and satisfaction we find in each freshly earned insight. That some of what we learn is probably wrong is just part of the fun. What seems to matter most in this clumsy process is the unpredictable interplay of what we're told with the revelations of what we discover on our own. Aldo

Leopold also said, "The only prudence in fishermen is that designed to set the stage for taking yet another, and perhaps a longer, chance."

Which is my way of saying that although any fishing book—including and especially this one—may not tell you many truly "new things," it should at least tell you a few. It should also give you a new look at many old things. And it should invite you to think about all these new and old things in your own way, so you can better make the experiment your own.

Paul Schullery
On Matthew Bird Creek, spring 2006

PART ONE

How Trout Take a Fly

Viator: *Oh, there was a bite!*
Piscator: *Yea, and a hit.*

WILLIAM SAMUEL, *THE ARTE OF ANGLING* (1577)

CHAPTER ONE

The River and the Bridge

The Yellowstone River first takes form south of the southeast corner of Yellowstone National Park, in the Bridger-Teton Wilderness of Wyoming. It is like any other high-elevation, steep-gradient stream those first miles: full of energy, low in nutrients, and in a hurry.

It works its way more or less north, through some of the wildest country on the continent. By the time it reaches the park boundary, it has been joined by other small streams and is a good-size little river. It is also as far from a road as it is possible to get in the lower forty-eight states. In the two dozen or so stream miles that it will now meander in that most remote corner of Yellowstone, it is joined by more streams until it spreads into its willow-blanketed delta and becomes Yellowstone Lake.

This is the largest high-elevation lake in North America—139 square miles of nearly uninterrupted wilderness shoreline, numerous small islands and a few large ones, and the home of a magnificent assemblage of wild plants and animals. It takes the water that enters Yellowstone Lake's Southeast Arm a full decade to emerge from the lake's outlet many miles to the north, and during those slow, patient years, the water is profoundly altered. The lake gathers the flow of more than a hundred tributaries, greatly increasing the size of the river it will soon again become. It slows and moderates the movement of all that water volume, evening out the more violent flooding cycles the upper river experiences. It acts as a settling basin, accumulating the silt of the higher-energy river and tributaries before sending the clearer water on its way, and it gives the water time to warm; both clarity and warmth make the Yellowstone River more hos-

At its delta at the southern end of the Southeast Arm of Yellowstone Lake, the Yellowstone River is still a relatively infertile high-mountain trout stream.

pitable to life. It is a mellower, richer river when it finally drains from its outlet and under Fishing Bridge.

The bridge ranks among the more interesting human structures in the park, especially for its place in the evolution of management of the park's ecological system. This is the second bridge to span the outlet in this general neighborhood. The original was built in 1902, and the present structure replaced it in 1937. At 532 feet long, with nineteen spans, the log trestle bridge connects the park's "grand loop" road with the East Entrance and the road to Cody, Wyoming.

Wildness

For the first seventy or so years of its lives, Fishing Bridge was the summer scene of an orgy of happily undisciplined recreational fishing. Tourists lined both sides of the bridge, casting all manner of lures and baits to the big trout below. These anglers were joined by many others in dozens of boats, underneath the bridge and upstream and down. It was a glorious mess, with a sizable catch of trout, ears, hats, and cars for its reward.

From the park's earliest years, fishing at the outlet of Yellowstone Lake was famous for almost unbelievable catches of the native trout. It was also

4

The decade-long moderating process of Yellowstone River water passing through Yellowstone Lake has transformed the river into the productive—and imperiled—trout stream we know today.

quick to suffer from the effects of overcrowding, which, besides including a good deal of social tension and piggishness, led to the gradual decline of the fish population.

There was a very good and unsavory reason that the fishing was outstanding here. The bridge squatted astride one of the premier spawning areas for Yellowstone cutthroat trout to be found anywhere in the West. Responding to that mightiest of biological imperatives, fish migrated to this area each spring from the lake, and others came from the river downstream, to participate in a wildlife spectacle of near-Alaskan proportions. That this was also a critically important stage in the existence of the trout population was of little concern to most visitors, but it gradually became of greater and greater concern to conservationists, managers, and quite a few anglers.

In the late 1960s and early 1970s, Yellowstone National Park underwent what was, by the usually stodgy standards of federal agencies, a revolution-

For more than thirty years, park visitors, whether anglers or not, have enjoyed the easy viewing of native cutthroat trout feeding, spawning, and living out their life cycles below the bridge.

ary change in management direction, aimed at increasing the "natural-ness" of the setting and reducing human influences on various popular wildlife species. I devoted significant portions of my books *Mountain Time* (1984), *Searching for Yellowstone* (1997), and *The Bears of Yellowstone* (1992) to this story, so I won't get into it here except to say that trout and trout fish-ermen were among those quickest to benefit from the new management regime, which emphasized restoration of native wildlife populations to the greatest extent possible.

Most important for my story, in 1973 fishing became illegal from Fish-ing Bridge and for a considerable distance both upstream and down. The long-beleaguered cutthroat trout were now secure to swim, spawn, and rise around the bridge. In that way, all at once a far healthier and more meaningful wildlife-viewing opportunity was added to Yellowtone's already fabulous wildland scene.

Finding My Way to the Bridge

I've been casually and haphazardly photographing wild fish for at least thirty years now—a few pictures of rising rainbow trout here, some gar in an Everglades pond there, steelhead in an Oregon river here, brook trout holding in a quiet Pennsylvania spring creek there. My first serious efforts occurred many years ago when I learned of a spawning run of brown trout on a small Montana stream with a formidable natural barrier to upstream migration. Here, trout had to leap through a foaming cataract several yards long to reach spawning waters upstream, and I spent hours standing only feet from the edge of the torrent, camera at the ready, clicking whenever I sensed motion. The results were mixed and included a great many pictures with sideways fish, parts of fish sticking out of the water or off the edge of the frame, or no fish at all. But of the thousands of nature photographs I've taken all over North America since 1970, few have so clearly portrayed the magnificent power of wild nature as did those lucky exposures that caught airborne trout arcing through the spray above that chute of whitewater.

I came to this enthusiasm for fish photography from two directions. In 1972, I started work for the National Park Service, in Yellowstone National Park, as a ranger-naturalist, a job devoted almost entirely to helping people better appreciate and understand nature. This same kind of work, whether I practiced it as a speaker, editor, writer, museum director, conservation activist, or in any other way, became and has remained a central focus of my professional life ever since.

The institution of special fishing regulations in the 1970s, most notably catch-and-release fishing and greatly reduced creel limits, made

A large brown trout jumping a cascade, Gardner River, Montana, in the 1970s. This stretch of stream has since reshaped itself, and the fish no longer need to make these heroic jumps.

Steelhead gather in a sheltering pool in Steamboat Creek, a key spawning area of the North Umpqua River, Oregon.

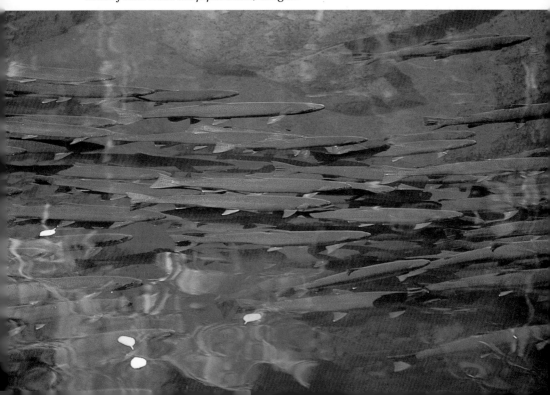

Tiny insects float over a big male desert pupfish, perhaps two inches long, in Salt Creek, Death Valley National Park. The pupfish challenges photography with the camouflage its ancestors evolved over many thousands of years for their entire population's existence in this single small creek.

Yellowstone something of a world model for coldwater fisheries managers and helped boost angler interest in wild trout management and conservation in many places. It was an enormously exciting time to be in Yellowstone, watching the effects of the new management policies from year to year. One of the leading figures in the redirection of Yellowstone aquatic resources management in those days was biologist John Varley, then assistant leader of the U.S. Fish and Wildlife Service project in the park. I learned much from him, and we recognized many overlaps in our interests and sense of direction for Yellowstone. Eventually he invited me to cowrite a book on the park's fish. We knew that an important component of our message must be fish appreciation—in short, we wanted everyone to realize that fish were wildlife. More broadly, we wanted nonanglers to gain a greater appreciation for what we considered a neglected element of Yellowstone's wild setting, which was why we called the book *Freshwater Wilderness* (1983). We devoted an entire chapter to the pleasures of fish watching, and throughout the book, we wrote about the fish precisely as we would have written about elk, bears, or any other wild animals.

The second source of my excitement about trout photography was fly fishing. Thanks to my big brother Steve, who loaned me a complete outfit, I began fly-fishing at the same time as I began working in Yellowstone. The sport soon filled in the spaces around several other pursuits or passions of mine, including American history, conservation, writing, photography, and natural history. In a sense, it actually helped solidify the tenuous connections among the others.

In 1977, I left Yellowstone to become the first executive director of the American Museum of Fly Fishing in Manchester, Vermont. Surrounded by the world's finest collection of the sport's crafts, with flies created by every great tier from the previous century to the present, rods made by every great builder of the previous two centuries, and books written by several centuries' worth of genuine experts, I began to write about fly fishing, especially its lore and history, but also about the conservation on which the sport depended. Eventually I published a few books that explored those subjects, and I became more and more intrigued by the long, slow growth of theory—all those complicated cultural conditionings, intellectual strivings, unexpected adventures, and empirical struggles by which we fly fishers have defined ourselves, our sport, and the trout.

I returned to the Yellowstone country in 1982, living for four years in Livingston, just north of the park, and then spent two years in southeastern Pennsylvania, where my job as a magazine editor was nowhere near as interesting as were the famous limestone spring creeks of that neighborhood. In 1988, I came back to live and work in the park and spent the next fifteen years there, learning, watching, and fishing my way through this wondrous landscape, becoming ever more deeply engaged by the beauties, stories, and cultural complications of Yellowstone.

So it was that between my enthusiasm for natural history and writing on the one hand and my absorption with fly fishing on the other, I was pretty well set up for what happened when I finally walked out on Fishing Bridge with a camera and started taking pictures.

Feeding Frenzies

I had intended to take pictures of the trout at Fishing Bridge since 1974, when I saw a friend's photograph of a few cutthroats holding over a deep green background of aquatic vegetation, the whole scene a study in sinuous golds and greens. Right then, seeing that lovely image, I knew I had to have one for my own. My imagined goal all those years was something like art: I wanted to capture as much of that beauty and motion and magic light as I possibly could and take it home.

The waters beneath Fishing Bridge provide a window into one of Yellowstone National Park's least appreciated ecological communities. In few other places in North America are people so openly encouraged to perceive and enjoy trout as wildlife rather than as sporting quarry or food.

I just never seemed to get around to it. I often stopped at the bridge and looked at the trout, and I always reminded myself that someday I had to get at it and take my Great American Trout Picture. But I suppose the reliability of the scene, year after year, so well protected there under the bridge—or so I thought, in the simpler days before whirling disease and other disastrous invasions threatened and still threaten to destroy this fabulous natural treasure—reassured me and forgave me the delay.

Then just a few years ago, my wife, Marsha, who was then the National Park Service's chief of public affairs in Yellowstone, needed to attend a meeting at a firefighters' camp near Fishing Bridge. I was on my own time that day, and I decided to tag along. I found myself with my camera gear, a couple hours to kill, and the bridge right within sight. I may be a little slow on the uptake, but I do know when the time has come.

It was about noon on a hot, bright day in early July. I walked out on the bridge and discovered that quite a few fish were feeding steadily on small mayflies and stoneflies. Eagerly rising trout are as exciting to me as the sight of a grizzly bear, and I was immediately caught up in the scene. Art for art's sake went straight out the window, and I went into my own little photographic feeding frenzy. Rather than looking for a fish tastefully holding over just the right color of bottom vegetation so I could get my evocative trout picture, I spent the next hour or so banging away at these eager risers from every angle I could manage.

If you're already a fly fisher, you know what happens when you come upon a scene like this. Even when you're not fishing, you feel a powerful need to engage the scene somehow. The camera was my way in.

As I was taking pictures, I wondered if my nice-but-none-too-fancy autofocus camera and 300-millimeter lens were up to the challenge of stopping the action. And I wondered what I might find when I could finally examine the pictures. I went from feeding frenzy to the suspense of waiting for the film to be processed.

What I found was as exciting as watching the risers. Of those first couple hundred slides, a surprising number weren't just blurry splashes; the camera had stopped the action at many distinct stages of the rise and take. What was just a quick flash of action when I watched it was revealed as much, much more. The more I looked, the more I saw. The more I saw, the more I needed to go back and take more pictures.

Perhaps the biggest surprise—almost a joke, really—was that I had inadvertently discovered that the best time to take pictures of these trout was the worst time by the standards of most wildlife photography. Photographers like the richly saturated and moody light of dawn and dusk, not the glare of midday. During my outings on Fishing Bridge, however, the sunlight came straight down onto the water.

But I wasn't after art; I was after information. The great gift of all that light was a series of revelations—of subtle features in the surface of the river, of telling details in the behavior of the fish, and perhaps most surprising of all, of the distinct, halo-edged, powerfully diagnostic shadows on the streambed directly beneath the fish.

And because this was wild nature, which becomes more provocative and graceful the better we observe it, the pictures captured its beauty in a way I had not dreamed of in my most artful ambitions.

Each subsequent visit to the bridge led me back into the literature on angling and, perhaps more fruitful, the physiology of feeding fish. I would look through each new batch of pictures, notice something new, think about it until I wondered about something else, then look through my growing collection of slides again and again and again. I'm still not done looking, and the more I find, the more I realize I'm a long way from being done taking pictures.

Subsequent trips and the study they inspired have turned into the most exciting new part of my Yellowstone life since the late 1980s, when two biologist friends taught me the basics of long-distance wildlife observation and I ratcheted up my capacities as a passionate observer of the landscape and life in this special place. Now I had taken my own long-standing advice, so often given to others, about watching trout as carefully and appreciatively as we watch other wild animals. I had begun a whole new exploration of Yellowstone's freshwater wilderness.

CHAPTER TWO

The Take

If you've watched many nature films on television, there's a powerful image you will almost certainly remember. The scene is a tropical reef, some colorful submerged landscape replete with coral forests, sponges, and other exotica. The whole thing is near enough to the surface for sunlight to dapple its happy, travel-poster community of plants and animals. But off to the side, accompanied by a sinister soundtrack, you see the snout, or even the whole head, of some darkly porcine, heavy-jawed fish, shadowed patiently amidst the undulating vegetation.

Then a new camera angle reveals an innocent little creature—a tiny fish, a crusteacean, or some other tidbit of biological mobility—going about its day, with a peppy, cheerful soundtrack to evoke additional sympathy.

You know what's going to happen, but it's always startling anyway, because it happens so fast. The innocent little tiddler comes doodling along until it's directly in front of the big fish, then it's suddenly gone, and the fish, which hasn't left its place, is closing its mouth. (Only the tackiest of producers put a small burp on the soundtrack at this point, but some do succumb to a little ascending pennywhistle toot to signify the hasty sucking in of the prey.)

It's a great nature film gimmick, always good for a chuckle. It's also terrifically interesting predatory behavior. It's evolution making the most of the animal's tools and environment. It's predation without the chase. It's always dramatic, and for all its staginess and comic effect, it's also a little scary. It looks almost like magic.

We don't hear much about this sort of thing with trout, especially those rising to feed near or on the surface. Their fastidious little riseforms, the spreading rings of ripples that follow each feeding episode, hint at a greater refinement, as if a trout has better table manners than to go around acting like a starship with an overactive tractor beam.

But trout use precisely the same suction forces as do the big reef fish. In a process that is likewise too quick for us to observe from the bank or even from a few feet away, they take in their food by means of a complex and forceful series of valvelike motions of surprising power and elegant efficiency.

Trout spent a long time getting this way. It seems likely that many millions of years ago, earlier forms of fish first developed the habit and ability to sift or strain huge quantities of water in through their mouths and out through their gills, at the same time developing some biological apparatus for capturing the variety of plankton and other small life forms that were in the water as it came through their heads. Some species of fish still do this today. But over time—long, generous, patient ages—given the specialization processes that animals so often undergo when the opportunity presents itself, sifting evolved into a more forceful process, and suction was added to the fish's feeding tool kit.

The organic mechanism that provides suction works both ways. Suction can be reversed, sending the fluids back the way they came. The capacity to move water at considerable velocity in or out of the mouth is common among fish; witness, to consider one extreme and startling example, the tropical archer fish that can spit water far enough to knock small insects from streamside branches.

When fishermen begin to learn about this process, it's predictable that they will pass through a stage in which they make a lot of jokes such as "The trout is really a sucker" and other comments of even poorer taste. So be it. But once you get used to the idea and run out of seventh-grade humor, you quickly see the wonder of how the trout makes its living. Then you start to think about what it might mean to your fishing.

The Path of the Prey

The photographs accompanying this chapter are all of wild, native cutthroat trout feeding in the Yellowstone River and have not been enhanced or altered except for some routine cropping at the edges. The fish, feeding quietly in the river, were not manipulated in any way, nor was their supply of food. I just photographed them as they fed on whatever came their way.

16

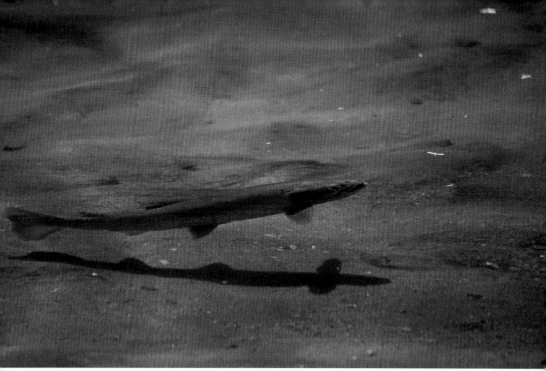

1. The trout can detect an approaching insect at a considerable distance simply by the dimpled disturbance in the mirrorlike underside of the water caused by the fly's feet or body. If the fly is struggling, has tipped over, or is otherwise active, the disturbance it makes is greater. But trout routinely seem to identify even quietly approaching flies at a distance greater than a trout's body length. At the point of recognition, the trout visually lines up the approaching insect so that its approach can be best viewed with binocular vision. The trout may wait for it or even move slowly forward toward it. Trout that are holding more deeply usually begin to move to the surface.

The photographs illustrate a trout's rise from beginning to end, but this portrait is a composite. The series includes pictures of several different trout, some taken from the side, some from almost directly above, and some from a considerable distance in front of the trout. This introduces a bit of uncertainty, because individual trout may not act like their neighbors. But in general, I think the composite portrait holds up well and provides essential aspects of the rise from different angles. The effect of that diversity of viewpoints is an unusually full portrayal of the trout's behavior during a rise. Any limitations caused by using photographs of more than one trout seem easily counterbalanced by the advantages of employing such a variety of perspectives. The captions that accompany the photographs complement this text.

Let's follow a mayfly to its doom in a trout's mouth, starting with the fly poised on the surface, riding the current downstream. A trout sees it and

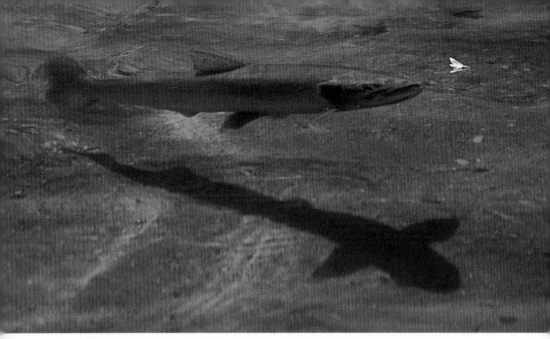

2. *Though the intense examination by the trout of this glowing mayfly dun is the most dramatic part of the photograph, it distracts our attention from the exciting reality that there are really three players on this stage: the trout, the fly, and the trout's shadow. All three have things to teach us about how trout feed.*

moves in to investigate. Forget for the moment that this one sentence encompasses a world of engaging wonders regarding the trout's visual acuity, its ability to identify prey, the refraction of light in a stream and how that affects the "window" of what the trout can and can't see as it looks up through the surface of the stream, and a host of other subjects that many fly-fishing writers have already quite capably explored. Right now, we're concerned only with the challenges the fish faces in eating this fly.

The best summary of the entire feeding process that I've seen was in a 1985 technical paper by biologist Neil Ringler. He divided the process of feeding into stages: detection (the prey is noticed); approach (the trout moves closer); fixation (the trout lines up to get the best bifocal look it can); inspection (the trout studies the prey, even drifting downstream under it for a moment); the attack (the trout swims quickly at the prey, sucks it in, and retreats) or the miss (alternatively, the trout fails to catch the prey); manipulation (the trout orients the prey in its mouth for swallowing); ingestion (the trout employs jaw motions and fluid pressures to move the prey to its throat) or rejection (the trout uses its fluid-forcing abilities to expel the prey). This is a formal outline of what the series of photographs shows a trout doing.

It seems safe to say that most of the time, the trout sees its prey, moves in, and promptly takes or rejects it. At least, that is what my own observa-

3. *Something about an individual mayfly sparks something in the brain of an individual trout, which turns from its feeding lane to investigate. In this case, the fly has tipped over and a wing is pinned against the water surface. Perhaps the trout's interest is triggered by the panicky motion of the insect's struggles, which send ripples of light and sound across the water. The trout I photographed often moved more than a body length to one side or the other to take a fly. Depending on the concentration of food in the current and the extent to which food is channeled into a tight stream or scattered across the surface, trout may range widely or feed exclusively in a narrow lane.*

tions, on many streams in many parts of the country, suggest. It's also what I hear from a number of well-traveled angling friends. And indeed, that is the simplest way it might happen. The fish approaches the prey, makes the decision to take it while moving in, and takes it without any noticeable hesitation.

But as anglers know, it isn't always that simple. Sometimes trout take longer to decide, and those trout are often the ones that the accomplished angler is most determined to catch.

Perceptive fly-fishing writers as far back as the 1930s described trout that would study a fly rather than just gulp it down, but Vincent Marinaro's beautiful book *In the Ring of the Rise* (1976), with its series of photographs of trout rising, gave anglers their first close look at some of the ways in which trout conduct their inspection of a prospective meal.

Water is a much thicker and potentially clumsier atmosphere than air. A fish that simply charges up to prey is likely to push its potential meal away with its own bow wave. But depending on the speed of the trout as it

4. *Even in the cleanest, clearest water, the trout must pick its food from a distracting assortment of flotsam in the surface film, caught here when the camera chose to focus on the film rather than on the trout below. Note in this photograph and the previous two that the trout has not yet aimed itself quite directly at the fly. It is still viewing the fly along a preferred line of vision across its snout. This behavior and its possible cause are further explained in an illustration on page 86.*

approaches the fly, the care it exercises, and the timing and intensity of the suction it uses, it may approach quite near. A fish can get its little face right up close to the insect and seem to lock its prey in place right there in front of it as the fly drifts along.

I wonder about this stage. Marinaro showed us, in his photographic sequences, the way a brown trout noses right up to a fly, then drifts backward along with it as the fly continues on its way downstream (the inspection phase of the take). The trout concentrates on the fly and keeps it right there, just up from and off the end of the fish's snout. This behavior is certainly agonizing for the angler, and who knows what the insect must make of it?

But here is what I find most curious. The whole time this is going on, often for several feet or even yards of drift, the fly is well within the suction range of the fish. In a scientific study by Johan van Leeuwen, he observed that rainbow trout feeding under the surface rarely applied suction toward food that was much more than a head length away. The photographs in

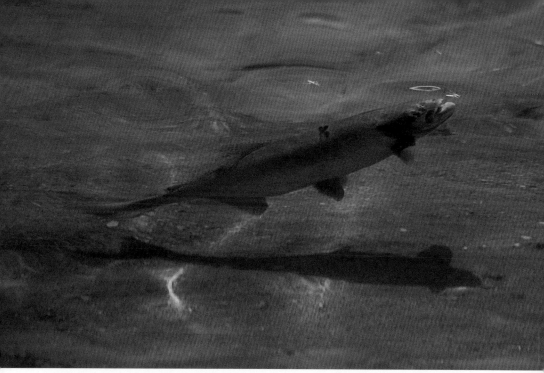

5. *With a mayfly spinner shadowing its back, this trout has a visual lock on another drifting mayfly. The fly is now well within the range of the fish's suction. The tiny lens of distorted surface just above the trout's head indicates that the fish has already begun to create a riseform, though whether it will take may still be uncertain.*

Marinaro's book seem to indicate that the distance at which his trout routinely inspected a fly was much less than a head length. So I must wonder whether the trout, while eyeing the fly from this close, isn't also applying some subtle little outward or inward currents to the fly, testing it in some way. Animals take every evolutionary advantage that comes along. Maybe the trout is only toying with the fly a little; trout are known to "play" with their food more toward the end of a hatch, when they are presumably sated, than at the beginning. Or maybe such manipulation, jostling the fly around a little, somehow helps the fish decide whether to eat it.

That's all speculation, but what happens next is vividly real. Whether the inspection is slow or quick, once the fish has approved the prey, it's time for the trout to feed.

Suction is the activating force. The goal of the trout is to create enough suction to ensure that the fly is drawn well into its mouth. To increase the force of that flow beyond its own physical capacity to create suction, the trout will move forward as it takes, its speed adding a little force to the current flow it is creating with suction and in fact allowing it to increase that suction and reach farther out with it.

6. *Here is the same stage of the process as in the previous picture, but with a different fish photographed from a different angle. The trout's mouth is slightly open, with the fly perfectly suspended across the gap. The lower jaw seems a bit underslung, probably because it is filling out as the fish begins to create the suction that will pull in the fly. The eyes are canted somewhat forward as the trout examines and targets its prey.*

There are now three distinct forces speeding the fly into the trout's mouth: the downstream flow of the current, the upstream movement of the trout, and the suction of the trout's mouth.

The trout creates suction by enlarging its mouth capacity, which it does by opening and extending its jaws, as well as dropping and widening the floor of the lower jaw, deepening the oral cavity. This is facilitated by pleat-like structures that run the length of the bottom of the lower jaw. With a cutthroat trout, these pleats keep the "cutthroat" marks partly hidden until they stretch open.

To tighten the stream of water being pulled in by the suction, the trout can reduce the extent to which it opens its mouth, creating a narrower, more precisely focused current. One disadvantage of this is that it requires more accurate targeting of the prey than a broader, if less concentrated, current would. A fish pursuing a stronger or larger prey, say a minnow or crayfish, may use the tighter current to move the heavier and perhaps fleeing prey back toward it. It is normally to the fish's advantage to get as close as possible to the prey before applying the suction, no matter what the prey is.

7. *The fly, in this case a mayfly spinner, has barely begun to tip into the opening mouth of the trout. Suction has also begun, and it appears that the beginning of the suction trough is passing over the head of the trout. On the stream bottom, the distorted light of the suction trough is beginning to obscure the shadow of the trout's head.*

The photographs clearly capture the effect of this suction. The surface-feeding fish, in sucking down the fly, actually pulls a shallow hole in the water surface, creating a little feeding depression, or trough. The insightful British angling writer G. E. M. Skues recognized the evidence of this process eighty years ago in *The Way of a Trout with a Fly* (1921), describing the initial stage of the take as "a faint hump on the surface, often accompanied by a tiny central eddy caused by the suction with which the trout has drawn in the fly."

In fairness to the incredibly elegant scientific studies that have been conducted with suction-feeding fish, I must assure you that my summary here is aimed at telling merely what I suspect anglers need to know for the narrow purposes of this book; there is a world of far more involved and fascinating information beyond that. If you are as enthusiastic as I am about the complex workings of fish, then you surely will want to know more. The trout's head and gills are in fact a sophisticated and amazingly adept valve system. I recently gave a talk based on many of these photographs to a well-educated audience at the University of Wyoming–National Park Service Research Center in Jackson Hole, Wyoming. Afterward, one of the people who came up to speak with me was a heart surgeon, who com-

8. *A frontal view now shows the mouth as open as it gets. A mayfly is in it, and two more drift by to the left. Again, note the forward angling of the eyes.*

pared some of the suction processes I had described to the way a heart pumps fluid through its valves. The hydrodynamics of suction feeding by a trout involves a surprising number of subtle actions and counteractions. I hope that by summarizing, I am not making things too simplistic, and I encourage you to check the references listed at the back of the book for more details.

But back to our trout, just now sucking down some insect. The fish's mouth has opened, the oral cavity has deepened, and the fly is either in or on its way into the mouth. The gills are already in play, as some water is moving out of them, but the fish is dealing with some involved physics at this point. If it simply drops the floor of its lower jaw and opens its mouth and gills all with equal force and at the same time, a lot of suction will still be created, but water will be pulled in from both ends—into the mouth *and* in through the gills. The latter, if it happens too dramatically, apparently is not an especially pleasant experience for the trout, and having both occur could defeat the goal of the suction. The trout needs to keep the suction going mostly one way, into the mouth, to have the best chance of capturing the fly. And even when the trout does this right, there may be a modest backwash into the gills, though not enough to interfere with the capture of the fly.

The trout's system of lips, oral cavity, and gills is sophisticated enough to do more than simply gulp in a big mouthful of water and then expel it

9. *It isn't enough to get the fly over the lip. It must be pulled deep into the fish's mouth, and the powerful suction is now doing that. The suction trough is clearly visible around the fish's head as down-curving distortion lines. The trough is likewise revealed in its shadow on the river bottom—a twin-lobed circle encompassing the trout's head.*

out through the gills. The amount of water that passes through the trout's head during a feeding episode may be considerably more than a mouthful, because the trout has the capacity to begin sending water out the gills while more is coming in through the mouth. Some of the photographs show this happening.

The forward speed of the fish is a key factor in increasing the through-head current involved in suction feeding. National Marine Fisheries Service scientist D. Weihs, in a review of studies of suction feeding by fish, concluded that a largemouth bass could increase the range of its effective suction of prey by more than 60 percent with enough forward swimming speed. No doubt that flashy, little last-second surge-and-turn maneuver that trout so often perform when they take a fly is in part an exercise in the same technique.

So now the trout has the fly in its mouth. But recall what anglers dread at this stage: that the fish will reject, or "spit out," the fly. Rejection of the fly is involved enough to need a chapter of its own, so for now let's assume that the trout approves of the fly. It closes its mouth and flushes the rest of the superfluous water out the gills while retaining the fly, presumably on

10. *The stage of strongest suction, viewed from the front, again reveals the circular trough in the short lines of surface distortion around the mouth. It is unclear what this trout is eating, though it resembles a fuzzy seedpod of some sort.*

11. *The distortion lines of the suction trough are somewhat less defined here, but the two-lobed shadow of the trough stands out on the river bottom. The twin-lobed shape is probably the result of the trout's chin and snout dividing the suction trough. At this stage, though the gills may be partly open, they are not fully expelling water.*

12. *Though the fish is somewhat obscured by the distortion of the water, this is the busiest picture in the sequence. The lower jaw is still distended, and the cutthroat markings stand out. Both gills are now open wide, with the right one clearly expelling a strong current of water. Water may also be exiting the left gill, but the light is from the right, as the off-center shadow of the suction trough on the river bottom shows, and the distortion of light on that side is probably lost under the fish.*

the tongue, in the throat, or against the gill rakers, those hard, arching structures to which the gills are attached.

So far, I haven't found a lot of precision in the scientific discussions of how the fish arranges to keep the fly from just squirting out the gills with the water. When you look into the oral cavity of a fish that's been feeding heavily on small insects, you will see them scattered around in there, many in the gullet, but others lodged here and there and not yet on their way down the throat. Presumably, through a combination of jaw and tongue movements, along with internal sloshing and sorting with water, the trout eventually gets most or all of them into its throat.

Predators

Setting aside for a moment what all this observation and photography and reading have taught me about fishing, they have given me a deepened respect for trout—creatures I already admired pretty thoroughly. Perhaps most important, I admire them much more as individuals than I used to.

13. *In this remarkably lucky photograph, the trout has closed its mouth, and the rapidly expanding suction trough is sliding back over its head. Most important, the quick closing of the mouth and contraction of the floor of the jaw are expelling water from the gills with such force that some of it also escapes in strong, little spurts from the sides of the fish's mouth. This startling process occurred with more than one of the photographed trout.*

The feeding process is so full of opportunities for variation—not only in one fish, but from one fish to the next—that I am much less likely than before to make assumptions about one fish based on what the fish next to it has been doing.

The scientific studies of trout feeding behavior leave little question that the variations I have casually observed among trout are not uncommon. Consider, as Robert Bachman has in his *Trout* magazine article "How Trout Feed," merely the variations that might be caused just by the relative locations of several fish in one reach of stream:

> If it is generally true, as I suggest, that trout in streams don't move about very much in search of food, then the food that passes by a trout in one feeding station may be very different from that of one stationed a few yards away. A trout at the head of a big pool may experience a very different food supply than the one in a small pocket or riffle. This would at least explain why sometimes one fly will work for one fish, while another will ignore it entirely.

28

14. *An equally lucky photograph captures an air bubble expelled from the trout's right gill just as it reaches the surface. As first noted by G. E. M. Skues in the early twentieth century, a surface-feeding trout inadvertently inhales air along with any fly. This air is then expelled out the gills with the water. My photographs suggest that, because the trout is usually in the process of turning and twisting downward to one side or the other as it expels the air, the bubbles usually all emerge from the gill on the trout's high side. Most of this trout's shadow is now lost in the distortion caused by the suction trough as it expands and becomes what we call the riseform.*

Each fish we watch or cast to has its own agenda and unique way of fulfilling it. Every rise is at least a little different. Sometimes it's very different.

In *Fisherman's Fall* (1964), Roderick Haig-Brown commented on this, saying, "I often wonder why, when we are so anxious to give our quarry credit for cunning, intelligence, even wisdom, we are so reluctant to admit that he may have individuality." We fishermen have made so many jokes about how these simple little creatures make fools of us that we have begun to believe not only that we're fools, but also that trout really are simple. They may not be as individualistic as humans, but I'm now convinced they're a lot closer to it than I used to think.

I also admire them more as predators. I don't know what's going on in a trout's head when it noses up against a fly, judging and deciding. But the more I stare at these pictures of fish staring at insects, the more I respect

15. *A trout settling almost straight down into the water, rather than turning to one side or the other, may emit bubbles from both gills. Most of the air bubbles from this trout's rise have already appeared and are drifting back over the fish as it settles back into its holding position. But one last fine stream of small bubbles can be seen, still underwater, as they emerge from the trout's right gill.*

whatever it is that the trout is going through. Like its physiological attainments, which result from millions of years of evolutionary engineering, the trout's cognition seems to me a spectacularly successful tool.

During my many years in the West, I've spent hundreds of hours watching predators, from the largest to the smallest, go about their work—conducting their assessments, passing their fateful judgments, making their perfect moves. I've seen packs of wolves chase and pull down elk. I've watched grizzly bears crisscross a mountain meadow until they spook up a bedded elk calf, then run it down and feed it to their cubs. I've observed coyotes and hawks mousing and osprey, eagles, otters, and brown bears fishing. And like every fly fisher, I've watched that most brilliant of predators, the swallow, exercise its aerial precision above countless trout waters, whacking the mayflies and midges at a rate any trout in the river would envy.

Predation is energy transfer at its most obvious. Though not always an easy or pleasant thing to watch when it happens among big brown-eyed animals we adore, it is somehow what I have been waiting and hoping to

16. *A single bubble, still flattened by its ejection from the trout's narrow gill slit, slips along the trout's side as it rises to the surface. The rings of the swiftly dissipating riseform are perfectly echoed on the stream bottom in front of the trout.*

witness most of the time on many days afield. Predation is life, and predators are what most animate this great western ecosystem that I call my home.

Trout are unmistakably members of the same guild. They are not "just fish." Trout are extraordinarily successful products of spans of evolutionary time I can barely comprehend, they are wondrous animals, and what they do is beautiful beyond words. Whatever rarefied sphere of consciousness or even wisdom these creatures may inhabit, and whatever we may eventually conclude about the primitiveness or sophistication of their brains, I am infinitely more aware of their superiorities than their limitations.

CHAPTER THREE

Reading the Rise

For me, any history of the angler's awareness of the trout's rise and the disturbance that rise makes on the surface of the water must begin with the great American artist Winslow Homer. His paintings of Adirondack trout-fishing scenes in the 1880s and 1890s bring the ethereal beauty of a trout's rise so perfectly and vividly to life that we anglers instantly recognize Homer as one of us—just another fly fisher, captivated as we are by that rapidly spreading silver ellipse that we spot, with a sudden intake of breath, as we scan the quiet water of a stream or pond at dusk. Just as artists have never improved on Homer's portrayals of an airborne fly line, they have never improved on his rising trout.

In Homer's watercolor *Canoeing in the Adirondacks* (1892), a guide and his sport canoe along the shore of a forested lake in the dim light; morning or evening, I don't know, but I like to think it's the end of a long day. Homer captures them just as they look back over their shoulders at a small, bright ring on the water. The sport's hand grips the gunwale, and the guide's paddle seems motionless. It is as if the sound of the rise caused them both to pause and turn, perhaps already considering whether to swing around for another go at that spot. No rod is visible in the canoe; maybe this scene depicts one of those days when the fish are rising and we're not ready for them.

I wonder how many nonangling admirers of Homer's art have looked at this picture and not realized that the trout's rise is the focus of the scene. If you aren't tuned in on what those little silver circles mean, you might just think the two men are vaguely gazing off in the distance, enjoying the scenery back the way they came.

Canoeing in the Adirondacks, *1892. Watercolor over graphite on paper, 15 1/2 by 20 inches, the McGlothlin Collection, courtesy the Virginia Museum of Fine Arts.*

In *Sunrise, Fishing in the Adirondacks* (1889), a lone angler's high, wide-looped backcast line carries glints of coming daylight, but except for a faint glowing trail of disturbed water behind his canoe, the foreground scene is almost black but for two bright rise rings. In *Casting, "A Rise"* (1889), the entire picture is the muted monochrome of near dark except for the wake of the angler's boat and, again, the spreading circle of the rise toward which he is casting.

Again and again, Homer captured that instant perfectly. The trout has just risen to take a fly, and the gently agitated water at the center of that small act of violence has begun to spread in those rolling silver ripples that fly fishers can watch thousands of times without a loss of magic. In a few seconds, the rings will dissipate and fade back to the uniform dark of the pond surface. But for just for a moment, they catch the slanting light—and our excited attention.

The riseform, which the great fly-fishing theorist Vincent Marinaro called "the final act in what may be, many times, a very complicated process," is both announcement and invitation. Final act it may be, but it is also a promise—of another rise, one in which we will participate more

Sunrise, Fishing in the Adirondacks, *1889. Watercolor on wove paper, 34.3 by 52.2 centimeters (sheet), Fine Arts Museum of San Francisco, museum purchase, Mildred Anna Williams Fund (1966.2).*

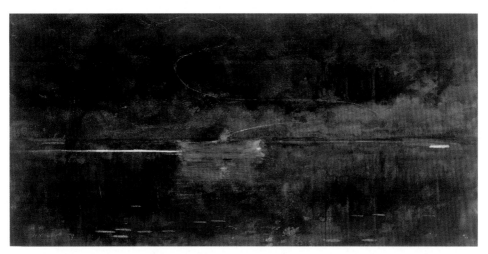

Casting, "A Rise," *1889. Watercolor on paper, 9 by 20 inches, Adirondack Museum, Blue Mountain Lake, New York (67.058.01).*

directly. It is our most urgent visual link to the trout's world. It is as close as trout come to leaving tracks.

What Homer's masterpieces remind me of is that for all our technology and advanced understanding of stream entomology, we modern fly fishers still aren't better streamside observers than our ancestors were. If it weren't for my camera, I would be no more capable of discerning special characteristics of a trout's rise than anyone before me. Homer stands for many generations of anglers before and since his time who were capable of looking hard at trout water, understanding what was going on, and making the most of it. The difference with Homer was that he was also a brilliant artist through whose genius we can see his trout rising as clearly as we see our own.

The Curl Occasioned

Fly fishers have been aware of the trout's rise and its effects on the surface of the water for a very long time. This is one reason why I have complained that angling history has been mistakenly portrayed as a great march of progress, from those kind-of-dumb-but-likable guys of the olden days up to us really smart guys of today. In fact, many generations ago, our predecessors were at least as smart as we are—or as dumb, for that matter—and many of them may have had more stream savvy than we do.

Two, three, or four hundred years ago, if anglers wanted to learn about trout, they were most often on their own or else dependent on a few friends or relatives for advice and guidance. There were some books around, if they could read and could find or afford them. But I think it's safe to say that many anglers didn't have much contact with those books, and that wasn't all bad. As angling historian Ken Cameron has put it, earlier fishermen had not yet begun "living in each other's intellectual pockets. Such people existed in a different informational atmosphere, one in which the low level of communications forced self-reliance."

Unfortunately, all those generations of unlettered local experts are the very ones we now know the least about. This is the reason angling historians get so excited when someone discovers some faded old fishing manuscript, a nineteenth-century angler's journal, or a centuries-old fly book with notes on when and where fish were caught on each fly pattern.

But for all the shortcomings of the information that has been left to us, we are still blessed with a wonderful literary legacy. And I suspect that in the case of the trout's rise, it's safe to say that what these more literate gents discussed in their writings in the centuries before ours was probably not much different from what their countless less bookish associates were also experiencing and talking about among themselves.

The fully developed riseform, its bubbles indicating a likely surface-feeding episode, epitomizes the mystery and excitement of fly fishing.

Alfred Ronalds, whose *Fly-Fisher's Entomology* (1836) is regarded as the foundation document of that field, identified the "curl occasioned by the rise" as the target toward which the angler should make his cast, "but should the undulations have nearly died away, before he can throw to the spot, then he should throw, as nearly as he can judge, a yard or two above it, and allow the flies to float down to the supposed place of the fish." Ronalds was often casting more than one fly, but I don't doubt that some of these flies floated on or in the surface of the water.

Even in Ronalds's day, other fishermen recognized that the "curl occasioned by the rise" was, from the very instant of its formation, moving downstream of the fish's mouth. Using the riseform to target your cast, in other words, would result in your fly landing behind the fish's head—too far downstream for best effect. Besides, casting right on top of the fish could easily scare it.

Thus George Bainbridge, whose *Fly Fisher's Guide* (1816) was one of the books that actually preceded Ronalds's with illustrated catalogs of important trout-stream insects, said that "when a Trout is observed to rise of his own accord, the flies must not be thrown directly over him, but about a yard higher in the stream, so that they may float down to his view, without the fear of agitating the water." Bainbridge apparently was concerned with not spooking the fish more than with making sure he compensated for the downstream movement of the riseform. So was Sir

37

Humphrey Davy, who, in *Salmonia* (1828), not only recommended throwing "at least half-a-yard above the fish," but also said you should make your line-lengthening false casts "in another part of the water" to avoid spooking the fish. It's clear that these writers were fully aware that rising fish could be quite shy.

Davy made other uses of the riseform. He said that an experienced observer could actually determine, "from the size of the tranquil undulation that follows their rise," the size of the fish he saw rising. "Reading" the rise has long been something of an art in itself.

Sips, Smuts, and Bulges

But it remained for the great angling formalizers of the late Victorian era, roughly 1870 to 1900, to attempt a thorough codification of this crucial but short-lived bit of angling evidence. In the final decades of the nineteenth century, fishing, like so much else in British society, was becoming more cosmopolitan. And it was more often practiced by urbanites who lacked the leisure of generous stretches of time by the stream that their predecessors enjoyed.

This change in the angler wasn't a simple upgrading of his tackle or his smarts. There had always been competitive and fiercely inquisitive fishermen, but the nineteenth century saw the triumph of the fly-fishing overachiever as the self-appointed judge of right and wrong in the sport's code. Swept along by the progress-oriented mood of an aggressively industrial society, these self-conscious sportsmen wanted different rewards. Many of them sought not so much the Waltonian joys of extended sporting jaunts in idyllic rural settings as the hastier joys of coached expertise in a tightly defined sporting arena.

This was entirely their choice, of course, and you and I are direct beneficiaries of all the fresh thinking to which it led. But I must admit that the Victorian gentleman anglers do remind me of so many of us today, who show up at the stream anxious to have the guide—our modern equivalent of the old rural angler who stayed behind to live the riverside life—settle the questions of fishing location, tippet size, fly pattern, cast, and the rest. We now can simply sidestep all those deliberations and start casting where the guide tells us to, with a fly he handed us, for a fish he correctly assures us is there. Sounds to me as if something has been lost.

But under this new intellectual regime, several centuries of loosely defined practice and local techniques were subjected to rigorous scrutiny in an ambitious, exciting, and sometimes arrogant attempt to standardize the informal traditional practice of a sport into a rigid and enforceable code. In the process, fishing technique and theory advanced substantially, individual creativity was channeled in certain directions, the pace of book and periodical publishing was dramatically accelerated, and no end of older techniques and individual flexibility were marginalized or even forgotten—or just quietly went on along less celebrated streams, among less socially ambitious anglers.

Inevitably, there were reactions against such restrictive formality, and the history of fly fishing since that time has in good part been the story of debates and competitions among champions of various theories and approaches.

Right or wrong, we do owe this change in fly fishing our gratitude for important advances in tackle and techniques. Among many other things, it was this heightened urge to define, categorize, and codify that led to big changes in how we dealt with and understood feeding trout.

The most significant element of the new formality was, by all accounts, the dry fly. Though for centuries many anglers had, when they needed to, caused their flies to float on or in the surface, dry-fly fishing was a more precisely defined practice involving certain kinds of flies tied specifically to enhance their flotation, cast in certain ways—only one fly at a time, upstream, and only to a rising fish—in more precise imitation of specific known aquatic insects. If no trout were rising, the most serious dry-fly fishers simply stopped fishing.

Though he was far from the first to practice this kind of fly fishing, the man now seen as the father figure of the dry-fly movement in England was Frederic Halford, a confident angling theorist, concise and engaging writer, and fly fisher perfectly positioned to advance the cause of understanding the way trout rise and feed. He discussed rises briefly in his first book, *Floating Flies and How to Dress Them* (1886), but it was in *Dry-Fly Fishing, Theory and Practice* (1889) that he devoted a long, thoughtful chapter to this subject.

Much more than any writer before him, Halford emphasized that the trout fed not merely by coming up to the surface and grabbing a fly with its mouth, but by actively sucking it down. The take was not a grab; it was a pulling suction. Whatever specific motion or approach the trout made as it attacked a fly, suction feeding was key to its success. I am not certain from his writings that even Halford realized how important suction was, but he did seem to have a finer sense of it than his predecessors who wrote about it. Oddly enough, the significance of this suction is still little appreciated among anglers today, which is yet another reason why Halford makes for rewarding reading more than a century after he wrote his best books.

In *Dry-Fly Fishing*, Halford ran through the basics that would be covered a hundred times by later writers. It is virtually impossible to separate a study of trout feeding behavior from the study of the riseform. Even the

OBSERVATION POND EMPTY.

OBSERVER DESCENDING INTO OBSERVATION CHAMBER.

The British naturalist Dr. Francis Ward pioneered underwater photography as a means of studying the behavior of several freshwater fish species. His specially constructed fishpond with built-in observation window provided him with a comfortable view of fish activities previously seen only poorly from above the surface. From Francis Ward, Marvels of Fish Life *(1911).*

dry-fly fisherman, concerned only with fish feeding on the surface of the water, had no choice but to understand all the ways in which fish feed.

Halford explained why. An apparent rise, revealed by some swirl or other upwelling or disruption of the surface currents of a stream, could indicate a fish that was actually feeding on floating insects on the water's surface, but it also could be a disturbance caused by a fish that was bulging (taking nymphs right below the surface), tailing (feeding head-down on stream vegetation or the streambed, with its tail breaking the surface), smutting (taking tiny midges or other "curses" with the tiniest of perceptible dimples on the surface), or minnowing (chasing smaller fish). It was up to the angler to sort out the possibilities and make the most of the realities.

Halford, like any good naturalist, observed with more than one of his senses, and the rise provided such an observer with some intriguing information. Unlike Davy, he evidently preferred to judge the size of a fish not so much by the shape or pattern of its riseform, but by the noise of the rise. He believed that the trout's "comparative weights may be said roughly to be arranged in a scale of harmony, the heaviest fish being the lowest bass, and the smallest the highest treble."

That wasn't all. If the pitch of the sound gave you the fish's size, the volume of the sound gave you the size of the insect it was taking: The bigger the bug, the louder the rise.

Most of what Halford wrote in 1889 is still regarded as valid, but his was only the opening round in an ever-intensifying effort to quantify this difficult-to-analyze and frustratingly ephemeral moment in trout natural history. Some of the photographs in Francis Ward's fascinating books *Marvels of Fish Life* (1911) and *Animal Life under Water* (1919), taken from a special windowed underground chamber constructed along one side of a pond, were quite revealing of how the riseform worked; *Marvels of Fish Life* contained what were probably the first photographs of a trout's riseform as seen from underwater. Other British dry-fly writers were considering the same questions in the 1890s and early 1900s, but the next significantly finer analysis of the rise—and the one that still seems most important of all— came from G. E. M. Skues.

Winks and Whorls

George Edward Mackenzie Skues was described by modern British fly-fishing experts Brian Clarke and John Goddard as "the greatest liberator of the human mind in fly fishing this century." During a forty-year period, starting with his book *Minor Tactics of the Chalk Stream* (1910), a work that earned him the title of the father of modern nymph fishing, Skues

The master British angler G. E. M. Skues is widely regarded as perhaps the most insightful angler-naturalist of the past century. His studies of riseforms codified most of the variations recognized today. This illustration by Marsha Karle is from a photograph in T. Donald Overfield's G. E. M. Skues: The Way of a Man with a Trout *(1977).*

was perhaps the foremost British fly-fishing writer-theorist. He also frequently corresponded with his American fly-theory counterparts, despite the different directions their own theories were taking them. Through much of his angling career, he symbolized the enthusiasms of the wet-fly fishermen in a long and often quite nasty debate with dry-fly fishermen over just what was appropriate practice in fly fishing.

The dry-fly versus nymph and wet-fly controversy on Britain's chalkstreams is a wonderful, perplexing episode in fly fishing's social history. It is hard for the American fly fisher, with the abundance of public waters and fishing techniques available to us, to imagine that these earlier British dry-fly enthusiasts could be so belligerently convinced of the singular rightness of their method. Not only did they sometimes ban any sort of subsurface flies from this or that private water, but some of them did not even regard such techniques as fly fishing. To us today, they appear as bigots. To themselves back then, they appeared as people protecting something fine and pure. But then, that is what bigots always think.

Like Halford, Skues counseled intense observation. When challenged on the difficulty of hooking a fish on a nymph cast upstream, he pointed out that, contrary to common imagining, the careful observer had a good chance of seeing the fish roll or twist to take the fly. He said that the angler should watch for a faint flash of light, which he immortalized in light-hearted "doggerel" as the "little brown wink under water":

I care for no trout that comes up with a splash
To capture the fly that I've brought her;
   Let the trout that will dash
   At my fly with a flash,
But tip me the wink under water.

In *The Way of a Trout with a Fly* (1921), Skues refined and advanced Halford's explication of trout feeding habits to almost as great an extent as Halford had improved on all those who preceded him. It was Skues, for example, who seems first to have realized that the bubbles one sees in a dissipating riseform were diagnostic proof that the trout was indeed taking an insect on the surface. If the trout took an insect just below the surface, it would have no air to eject through its gills. Only if it had fed on the surface and sucked in air along with the insect could it eject the bubbles into the riseform. This assumed that the fish did not generate the bubbles through the turbulence of the rise, with its dorsal fin or tail, for example; but on Skues's quiet chalkstreams, rises were sedate enough that such turbulence was thought unlikely in most feeding situations.

Skues most distinguished himself in his quest to understand the rise by further refining Halford's narrative into a list of about a dozen different rises that resulted in either actual riseforms or other surface disturbances. These ranged from the mildest surface disturbance to the most pronounced—from the various "bulges" that fish made on the surface as they fed on mayfly nymphs and emerging caddis that were still underwater, through the slightest "smutting" or "sipping" rises to small insects on the surface (a small rise didn't necessarily indicate a small trout), to the more showy rises to larger flies, and on to the "slash" at caddis moving actively on the surface and even the "plunge," in which the fish "comes almost entirely out of the

G. E. M. Skues's famous kidney-shaped whorl, which he believed was the distinctive riseform trout created when feeding on certain British "olive" mayflies. Clarke and Goddard later declared it nonexistent. That one leading authority could speak so confidently and descriptively of a riseform that other leading authorities would insist didn't even exist suggests past difficulties with fine-scale interpretation of riseforms. From Taverner, Trout Fishing from All Angles.

A "bulging" trout, as pictured in Eric Taverner's Trout Fishing from All Angles *(1929), was said to result from a trout turning laterally rather than downward after catching a nymph right under the surface. Taverner elaborated on the nature of this rise: "The swirl rises to the surface as a crinkling of the water, which is known as a bulge, a sort of influorescence reminiscent of the top view of a cauliflower."*

water and takes the fly either as he leaves the water or as his head re-enters it." Among Skues's most appealing and enduring observations was his recognition of a common riseform, the result of the trout's peculiar enthusiasm for certain species of mayflies, which caused the fish to take those species with an eager swirl that he called the "kidney-shaped whorl."

British fishing writer Eric Taverner expanded substantially on Skues's list of rises and riseforms in *Trout Fishing from All Angles* (1929), raising the total to sixteen or more, depending on how you count his variations on certain rises. He discussed each at some length and illustrated a number of them with nice line drawings. Among other things, Taverner has been credited with originating the term "rise form," which he first used in an earlier book, *Divers Ways to Tackle Trout* (1925).

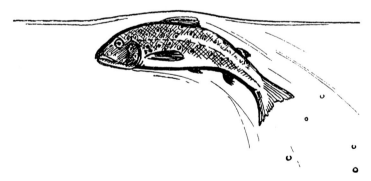

Taverner distinguished between "bulging" and what he called "humping," which occurred when a trout turned downward while catching a nymph. He said this motion "causes a sort of humping of the water without actually breaking the elastic skin of the surface. The water is seen to lift, stretch, and then to recede." Most modern writers, when describing this effect, would probably just refer to it as "bulging." From Taverner, Trout Fishing from All Angles.

Taverner illustrated a "tailing" trout, one "rooting with its nose in the weeds for nymphs and shrimps and keeping in an almost vertical position by flexions of its body." In fact, depending on water depth, trout may visibly "tail" at almost any angle and not just vertically. From Taverner, Trout Fishing from All Angles.

Fascinating natural history observation all this may have been, but it was really quite practically directed. The whole point of reading the rise was to determine what the fish were taking. Skues's and Taverner's lists of rises were, as precisely as they could manage, what we today might call a field guide, aimed at relating trout behavior and surface disturbance to fly-species presence. And between Halford's generalized discussion and the Skues-Taverner analytical approach, the British dry-fly fisherman had the likely options covered. Skues added some more notes on rises in *Side-Lines, Side-Lights, and Reflections* (1932), as well as a few helpful photographs of rising trout by J. Edwards Moss. Refinements were made by others, including a personal favorite of mine, *Fly Fishing: Some New Arts and Mysteries,* by J. C. Mottram (1915), but the fundamentals of understanding trout surface-feeding behavior and reading the riseform were now in place.

This is not to say that the conversation ended. *The Flyfisher & the Trout's Point of View* (1931), by Col. E. W. Harding, remains about the most rigorous popular examination of the subtleties of trout feeding behavior, replete with numerous graphs charting the progress of the fly on the surface of the water, the movement of the trout to intercept the fly, and the behavior of light on the trout's and the angler's perceptions of what is going on. Vincent Marinaro, who did so much to advance trout-fishing theory in America based on his studies of brown trout in Pennsylvania's

Letort Spring Run, readily acknowledged that Harding's book was "the most comprehensive of all . . . wherein the broad outlines of the whole subject are drawn for the purpose of study now and in the future." Among his other discussions, including fish and human vision, how trout perceive color, the physics of the water surface, and how a dry fly affects the surface, Harding elaborated on how and why the trout moved through the various rises, but had little to say about what each riseform looked like. It apparently seemed unnecessary to him to repeat or elaborate on the list of riseforms already identified by Skues and Taverner.

But by the time of Taverner, today's reader slogging dutifully through these earnest treatises will notice some awkward strain and torque in the rhetoric. The distinctions these experts told us to watch for were becoming pretty demanding for the average observer.

The disturbance of the water's surface has a life span of seconds. Its critical first stage, when its features are best interpreted, vanishes almost immediately. Even if there is a significant upwelling of water—what some early writers referred to as the "bell" of the rise—it collapses immediately, leaving only a generalized memory like many others.

Thus Taverner's "porpoise roll" and "head and tail rise," though in their own right poetically apt terms for known trout feeding behavior, seem mighty similar on paper and may be essentially alike under the fast and difficult viewing conditions on the water. His "sucking rise form," the "sip to a medium sized fly in an eddy," the "spotted ring," and the "sip rise" must have seemed to some readers even in his day more than a tad redundant. And his "pyramid rise," which resulted in "the projection of a column of water upwards and at an angle with the surface of the water," the "slash," and the "leap" were perhaps easily distinguishable by Taverner, but for the purposes of most fishermen, they would probably fall under the more general heading of a "splashy rise."

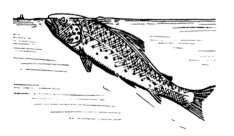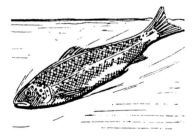

The "head and tail rise-form," according to Taverner, concluded with a "satisfied wag" of the tail slightly breaking the surface of the water. From Taverner, Trout Fishing from All Angles.

The "porpoise roll," a smoothly arching motion by the trout in slow water, was thought to indicate feeding on spent spinners. From Taverner, Trout Fishing from All Angles.

Taverner said that the "pyramid riseform," a "projection of a column of water upwards and at an angle with the surface of the water," indicated a more energetic rise, often to hatching "sedges" (caddis). From Taverner, Trout Fishing from All Angles.

I don't doubt that under the local conditions that Taverner described, he was able to exercise this sort of discernment, but the broad applicability of such terminology was and is problematic. By Taverner's time, I suspect, the theoretical edifice was getting a bit bloated for practical purposes.

Or at least, that seems to be the judgment of most later writers. Almost fifty years after Taverner published his list, Ernest Schwiebert's encyclopedic *Trout* (1978) did set a record for the greatest number of distinct riseforms described, cataloging about twenty, including all of Taverner's and a few more. But otherwise, a more conservative approach has prevailed, and most writers have listed only a few basic kinds of riseforms.

Fast Water

One reason for a more moderate and generalized approach to riseform description may have been the perceived limitations that many American writers felt they faced in trying to describe the rise on their waters. The dry fly, which since Halford's time has been the primary impetus for the study of riseforms, had a far broader destiny than remaining the exclusive domain of the British chalkstream fishermen.

Between the mid-1880s and 1915, the dry-fly writings of several British writers, including John Harrington Keene, R. B. Marston, and Halford himself, were serialized in American sporting periodicals, and new British dry-fly books became readily available in the American market as soon as they were published. Americans noticed. In the 1880s and 1890s, American tackle companies began to carry Halford's dry-fly patterns for American anglers to buy and use. Several American fishing writers, perhaps most notably among them Theodore Gordon, George LaBranche, Samuel Camp, Louis Rhead, and Emlyn Gill, picked up the banner of the dry fly. By 1915, the year of Gordon's death, Gill, Camp, and LaBranche had all published books on dry-fly fishing as it should be practiced in American waters.

Judging from the content of this literary output, the Americans had far less interest in dissecting the finer points of the rise. From the beginning, they set up a dichotomy that, though often true, was an oversimplification of immense proportions: that American trout streams were so different in character from the streams fished by Halford and Skues, being faster and rougher, that British techniques would need considerable adapting.

George LaBranche, in *The Dry Fly and Fast Water* (1914), by far the best of these early works and still among the most insightful of American fishing books, probably spoke for many of his colleagues when he summarily dismissed all the various bulges and tailings of trout from any consideration as being riseforms at all, because the trout did not actually "rise" to the surface. More important, he regarded the study of subtle differences of riseforms as unnecessary:

> Compared with our swift-flowing water, the gentle, slow-moving chalk streams of Southern England offer greater advantages to students of the habits of feeding fish, not only because of the greater deliberation with which the trout secures his food in them but also because a greater number of aquatic insects contribute to his sustenance there than are found on our swift streams; consequently, the English student has far greater opportunity for observation.

Right: *George LaBranche, one of America's most influential dry-fly theorists, was skeptical of interpreting riseforms. Unlike the British dry-fly anglers, who fished primarily on smooth-surfaced chalkstreams, he fished the rougher streams of the Appalachians, where subtle distinctions among types of riseforms were more difficult or impossible to detect. Louis Rhead's fishing portrait of LaBranche, which appeared as the frontispiece in Rhead's* American Trout Stream Insects *(1916), was hand colored by Marsha Karle.*

In order to make such a sweeping statement, LaBranche and his fellow American dry-fly pioneers were ignoring a great many American waters that were quite similar in character to the streams Halford fished. The limestone country of southeastern Pennsylvania, with its dozens of spring creeks, and similar waters across the United States all the way to California would indeed provide generations of angling theorists with "opportunity for observation" exceeded nowhere in England. This also explains why, when American fly fishers got serious about figuring out their spring creeks, they found the writings of Halford, Skues, G. A. B. DeWar, Harding, and their colleagues much more useful than the writings of LaBranche and other fishers of the American freestone mountain streams.

Besides the large number of accommodating American spring creeks, many of the freestone streams that LaBranche considered fast waters had a good deal of calm water. Emlyn Gill, in *Practical Dry-Fly Fishing* (1912), called these "glassy glides" and credited New York dry-fly angler and writer Walter McGuckin with the idea of fishing them. Gill thought that fishing such quiet water with a dry fly was, if anything, easier, because the fly was less exposed to the little waves and shocks that might sink it. But he also regarded such places as novelties rather than the main interest of the American dry-fly angler, and that seems to have been the consensus for the next few decades, until new generations of angler-naturalists confronted the challenges of the calm American waters.

I have wondered whether my own recent experiences successfully observing and photographing rising trout on a huge, quiet stretch of the Yellowstone River at seven thousand feet elevation in the Rocky Mountains would come as a surprise to LaBranche, who might have thought of the Rockies as home of even faster waters than were found in his gentle, old Appalachians.

The Modern Sensibility

By the 1930s, the trout's rise and the common riseforms were mostly defined. Ray Bergman, whose best-selling *Trout* (1938) serves as a representative example of fly fishing's mainstream at the time, kept his list of types of trout rises to nine. Most of these can be identified as matching the more generalized ideas of Skues and Taverner, though in some cases named differently, and I suspect readers were puzzled by Bergman's differentiation of the "splash" and the "slash."

There was still the occasional serious student of the rise in America or England, though. H. E. Towner Coston, a British writer and photographer who seems to have been utterly forgotten by angling society, published two books, *Beneath the Surface: The Cycle of River Life* (1938) and *Water Symphony: Fishing with a Camera* (1948), with a series of impressive photographs of trout holding in the water, approaching flies, and taking them in various riseforms. Both books include a photograph of the suction trough made by a rising trout in quiet water, when the fish pulls a shallow hole in the surface as it sucks in the insect, the most telling depiction I've seen of this phenomenon before I noticed it in my own photographs. Where is Coston's name in the ever-popular recitations of angling's theoretical pioneers?

Other new observers did make some interesting and important contributions to the lore of rising trout. Perhaps most notable in America were the books of Vincent Marinaro, *A Modern Dry-Fly Code* (1950) and *In the Ring of the Rise* (1976). Marinaro's observations in the second book, buttressed by his beautifully revealing photographs of feeding trout, added some previously undescribed types of rise behavior to the angler's lexicon: the compound rise, in which the trout drifts downstream along with the fly, apparently inspecting it for several feet of float or more, before taking or rejecting it; and the complex rise, in which the trout does the same extended inspection, begins to let the fly drift away, and then comes at it again and takes it. There are few more suspenseful moments for a fly fisher than watching a big brown trout in the midst of such deliberations.

During the times I have spent watching and photographing Yellowstone cutthroat trout rising to flies, I have yet to see one perform that same deliberative process. Once they were within suction range of the fly, they made the decision quickly to take or refuse each prospective food item they approached. The Yellowstone cutthroat is known, by reputation and from various studies done under actual fishing conditions, as a much more easily caught fish than the brown, but under the right circumstances, any trout can become more choosy and cautious. I've seen this, and a casual poll of some friends assures me that all the trout species do at times engage in the extended examination and delayed take.

My friend Tom Rosenbauer, author of several of the best modern books on fly fishing, recently told me about brook trout conducting these same long inspections on New York's historic Caledonia Spring Brook. These observations are especially interesting considering the brook trout's popular reputation as an easily caught fish.

> In the stream where I grew up learning fly fishing as a teenager (Caledonia Spring Brook, where Seth Green had his hatchery), brook trout were more abundant than browns or rainbows. Most of their feeding was on midge pupae and adults. When feeding on emerging pupae or adults, they would show just as long inspection stages as any brown trout. They

were also as selective as any brown trout, in fact more so. The browns did not rise as often, but when they did, usually on dark days, they were far easier to catch on a dry. I have seen the same behavior on the Battenkill. My theory is that the brookies in both streams were more practiced at surface feeding and knew exactly what they wanted, where the browns were rookies at it because they did not do it as often. Of course this is tempered by the overall greater spookiness of the browns, which I think leads people to believe they are more selective.

I've never fished Caledonia Spring Brook, but my five summers fishing the quiet upper reaches of the Battenkill in Vermont taught me never to assume that the rising brook trout would be more naive than other trout.

At least as interesting as Marinaro's descriptions of compound and complex rises, from a natural history standpoint anyway, was his description of a trout "gobbling" insects during a heavy emergence in very quiet water, when flies are dense on the surface. At the peak of such activity, the upper portion of the trout's head may stay above the surface of the water for several seconds as the fish noisily "gobbles" insects off the surface of the stream. Marinaro borrowed this term from the renowned British riverkeeper-writer Frank Sawyer.

I've had the good fortune to watch trout gobbling like this. My own observations of gobbling behavior on western spring creeks at first misled me into suspecting that this was a circumstance in which the trout had little use for suction, because the flies were so thick and the current so slow that the fish had only to hold in place, open its mouth, and let the river do the work of washing the flies into its mouth. But as Marinaro pointed out, the trout "lifts and falls on the clusters of insects like a man making rapid pushups. With each fall there is a peculiar sound that suggests that he is slapping the water with the roof of his mouth." This is not quite how I would characterize the sound I have heard in similar situations, which was more of a soft popping—a muted rendition of the champagne cork noise. In these cases, however, the trout may have been behaving somewhat differently in some minor element of its take. But I am reasonably sure that both sounds are the result of the fish using its customary feeding suction, again and again, except that it is happening in water quiet and still enough that the sound is not drowned out by the noise of running water or the splash of the rise.

It is these minor variations in trout behavior, no doubt complicated by differences in observer skill and terminology, that play havoc with attempts to speak definitively about trout rises. These fish live in such a wide variety of habitats and respond to such an imponderably huge array of local circumstances that it probably will always be hard to standardize our descriptions.

Side-by-side trout rising almost simultaneously create a confusion of patterns on the surface. The fish on the upper right further complicates the scene by giving the surface of the stream a swish or two with its tail.

Marinaro's *In the Ring of the Rise*, published just two years before Schwiebert's *Trout*, which contains the largest catalog of distinct riseforms in the history of the sport, has this broadly skeptical comment about rise-form interpretation:

> Unfortunately, the riseform, important as it is, does not tell the fisher-man very much, certainly not as much as he needs to know. It tells him only that a trout is feeding and in a few circumstances it may tell him what kind of insect is being taken. That is all.
>
> The riseform does not disclose to the fisherman the trout's observation or feeding station. It does not reveal the direction from which the rise came. It does not tell how far the trout drifted with the insect before the rise occurred, or on which side of his face the trout has been feed-ing, or whether he took the insect facing upstream, across stream, or downstream. There are many more questions to be answered.

Judging from what is said in most trout-fishing books and magazines these days, Marinaro's view of the riseform as an interesting and some-times helpful, but not always conclusive, bit of evidence prevails among modern anglers. Dave Whitlock, writing in the summer 2004 issue of *Trout* lists seven riseforms. One of these, the "flash," synonymous with Skues's "little brown wink," involves sighting a fish underwater without any sur-face disturbance. The other six—the swirl, hump, head-fin-tail, splash,

Fly fishers' studies of rising trout have been confined to the quietest waters of trout streams, especially that large class generally known as spring creeks or chalkstreams. Such places are among the most hospitable of trout habitats, with relatively constant environmental conditions, abundant vegetation, and slow, clear currents. Green Spring Creek, in Pennsylvania's famed limestoner country, presents an almost stereotypically perfect image of the lushness and beauty of such waters.

leap, and sipping rise—are surface riseforms and accurately reinforce the observations of earlier writers.

But after Marinaro's book, the lead in reconsidering the rise and the riseform promptly returned to the British, with Brian Clarke and John Goddard's *The Trout and the Fly* (1980). This book's color photographs were no doubt a revelation to many fly fishers, not only for the many interesting new angles on fly appearance in and on the water, but also for the helpfully diagnostic pictures of various types of rises and other feeding activity. And Clarke and Goddard far surpassed Marinaro in their entertaining and pointed discussion of how to interpret riseforms.

This field guide to reading the signs of feeding trout begins with "invisible" fish, with the authors emphasizing that fish that didn't leave any of the traditionally recognized water disturbances to indicate they were feeding still might be seen. A trout's motions while feeding, even if they made no easily noticeable impression on the surface, might still be read in faint distortions of reflections or even in slight breaks in the normal flow lines. In cases like this, Clarke and Goddard, much like Skues before them,

54

encouraged anglers to develop new and more exacting observational skills, especially "searching images" that would serve them when such subtle evidence was all that was available.

They reduced all riseforms caused by surface feeding to four: the "sip" or "kiss" rise, a quiet-water phenomenon resulting in a distinct sucking or sipping sound and a very small dimple on the surface; the "slash," a far greater surface disturbance caused by a trout moving at much higher speed to capture prey that threatens to escape; the "waggle" rise, in which the trout's whole upper side seems to push against the surface film at once as it feeds calmly on small flies; and the "plain rise," with no unusual motions or sounds, resulting in the typical circular riseform with a few bubbles in it. The fourth is the one we see most often.

The "waggle" is a curiosity in this short list worth a moment's historical digression. Here is how the authors described it:

> It is a languid rise: a rise clearly made by a fish that has had a good sighting of its prey, and that has simply drifted up into the surface from its position just below. It is a rise made by a fish that has almost lain in wait for the fly to drift into its mouth. There is the merest trace of forward propulsion as the fish, mouth closing and turning down from the horizontal, shrugs his way below the film again.

Clarke and Goddard then engage in some entertaining, if not necessarily convincing, anthropomorphism, citing an unnamed earlier authority who "described the languid shrug as 'a satisfied wag of the tail.'"

Ray Bergman's book *Trout,* which said that the "satisfaction rise" concluded with "a little wiggle of the tail," might be the original source of this pleasant notion. Bergman said this was a common rise among "the large selective risers in the Wyoming country," and like Clarke and Goddard, he unabashedly attributed it to the fish's gratification. I can't speak for the emotional fulfillment of the many Wyoming trout I've watched rise, but I will admit that it is pleasant enough seeing them slide gracefully back down after a perfect take to imagine that they are enjoying the trout's mental equivalent of a "life is good" euphoria.

Clark and Goddard discarded Skues's famous "kidney-shaped whorl" as a myth, stating that there was nothing in particular about the insect species involved that could possibly cause the trout to make a distinctive riseform:

> When a fish moves to intercept a fly, it displaces water. And it is true that there is a direct relationship between the speed of the fish, and the violence with which the water is disturbed. But the disturbance itself can and does take on almost *any* shape, give or take a broad circular movement that is influenced by the current, once the action is over.

Conclusions and Questions

With the advantage of a sizable and fairly recent scientific literature on suction feeding in fish, most of which has been published since the Clarke and Goddard book appeared in 1980, I started with a greater appreciation than most of these earlier writers for how much impact suction could be having on the riseform. This led me to reconsider some things, especially as my photographs accumulated and I could see not only patterns and consistencies, but also variations. It was a fascinating learning process for me.

For one thing, though it is only an academic question to anglers, at least since Skues's time, we have thought of the riseform as originating in some amount of upwelling of surface water as the fish swims up, feeds, and quite naturally causes the surface to bulge upward. But the photographs of the quietest of the rises showed that a trout was able to ease up to the surface with little or no bulge. The first noticeable change in the surface in these situations developed as the fish sucked in the insect. Thus the riseform began as a depression in the surface, the suction trough, rather than as a bulge. Coston's 1938 photograph of a suction trough shows this too. Either way, trough or bulge, the effect is the same: the spreading ripples of the basic, simplest riseform, slipping over the trout's back and dissipating downstream. But it was pleasing to understand the process a little better.

More practically, when I began to study my photographs of rising trout, one of the first things that struck me was the distinct individuality of each rise. To explain this, let me dismantle the process of the rise from another direction.

Anglers have long emphasized that the trout's feeding lane may vary tremendously. Many writers have commented on the very narrow lanes of exceptionally comfortable and well-fed fish, which will not move more than a few inches to either side of their stations to take floating insects. Other writers have described fish that were essentially cruising, ranging a foot here, a yard there, pulling down prey as if at random from the surface of a section of stream. The Yellowstone cutthroats that I photographed varied from individual to individual, depending on all the circumstances that affect such behavior, including quirky local currents, location in the water, presence and competition of other fish, abundance of prey, and water depth. But for the most part, the fish I observed fell between the extremes described above. They fed fairly close to the narrow bands of current they occupied but were often willing to swim a foot or more to either side and frequently did so. Those that were holding more deeply in the water may have ranged farther from side to side, but few if any showed strong fidelity to the sort of narrow feeding lane that seems to have characterized some of the trout described by Marinaro and others.

These trout were feeding steadily in clear, calm-surfaced water, and their food supply was abundant, with small mayfly and stonefly species steadily coming over in good numbers, but not so dense that a fish could feed constantly without some modest lateral movement. On some days, a trout might rise several times per minute and keep up that feeding pace for half an hour or more at a stretch.

Because of this wider-ranging foraging, they naturally approached the prey from many angles. Marinaro's comments on the limitations of the riseform and Clarke and Goddard's reconsideration of the kidney-shaped whorl were routinely proven correct by the trout I photographed. Fish approaching a floating insect from almost any direction within the half sphere of water below the insect, and doing so at a range of speeds and with different turns and lengthwise twists depending on the location of their holding stations and their chosen paths from it, were capable of an infinite variety of surface disturbances.

But the trout's approach to prey was only one factor in the creation of the riseform. The actual feeding episode, with its amazingly involved suc-

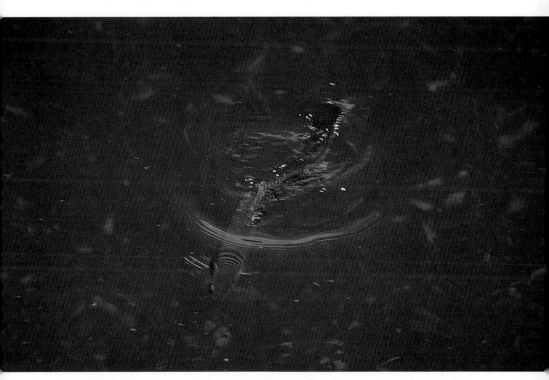

Not all bubbles are proof of a trout rising to a floating insect. In the postrise process of driving itself back to its holding position, a trout may create additional turbulence and bubbles with its dorsal fin or tail.

tion trough, surface bulge, and scattering spray—which can occur in surprisingly quiet rises, even though we don't necessarily notice the spray without photography—created surface disturbances that were anything but consistent in shape and size.

Each trout added a third set of potentially complicating disturbances to the surface as it turned down to go back to its holding station. These final disturbances included the turbulence generated by the turning motion of the trout's body, which was further complicated by the possible breaking of the surface by the dorsal fin or tail. Though it is true, as several experts have noted, that a trout's calmest, slowest rises are made to insects that are unable to escape, it is also true that trout taking even passive prey sometimes stir up the surface with the dorsal fin or tail. Thus the identification of bubbles in the riseform, though a likely sign of a fish genuinely feeding on the surface rather than just below, isn't a sure thing, because the trout's tail does sometimes generate adequate surface turbulence to create bubbles in the riseform.

One proof of the infinite range of small variations in the trout's rise and riseform is in the fish I've foul-hooked during my fishing experience. Over the years, I've accidentally snagged fish in pretty much every fin, the tail, and here and there on the body. This seems to indicate that the fish turned away from a fly or brushed against the fly and leader in a great many different ways, and it reinforces the point that there is great variability in the finest movements of the rise.

A significant difference between the trout I photographed and those observed in other studies was that these cutthroats did not always return to a precise location. In the relatively uncluttered environment of a large, open river with a smooth or deep bottom, holding stations tended to move around. Fish sometimes lined up in the laterally drifting seams of current that were created by the pilings of the bridge, no doubt taking advantage of some energy savings through a process similar to the way flying waterfowl are known to slipstream. Fish in shallower water found little or no advantage in holding in one specific spot, because the bottom in the whole area where I was photographing was generally uniform and thus the current was uninterrupted by rocks, logs, and other flow breakers.

This is one condition that differentiates my local trout from the brown trout described in the wonderful and far more rigorous studies conducted by Robert Bachman and associates in Spruce Creek, Pennsylvania, as well as the brown trout of New York's Neversink, about which Leonard Wright made less formal but revealing observations in *The Ways of Trout* (1985). Bachman's fish tended to show profound allegiance to certain energy-efficient locations relative to current obstructions, whereas Wright's showed equally powerful allegiance to shelter. Marinaro, in his observations and photography of Letort brown trout, seemed to concentrate on fish holding in very narrow feeding lanes, partly concealed or within escape range of heavy aquatic vegetation. My trout were not exempt from energy-saving concerns, but the circumstances of the bridge and river allowed them greater latitude in where they held in the current.

All the waters discussed by the various fishermen who have observed feeding trout have a common characteristic, though, which is the very problem faced by George LaBranche: We observe trout in quiet water, because that's where we can see them well. The kinds of distinctions that quiet water allows us to make among riseforms are much harder to make, and may be impossible, in broken water. The more broken the water, the more the riseform classifications tend to become obscured by the end-lessly interfering wavelets, troughs, and crosscurrents that prevail. It is here that the interpretation of the riseform probably offers the most chal-lenges, and perhaps also the greatest rewards, to the successful reader of such troubled waters.

Trout exhibit as many kinds of behavior as their environment demands. All of us who spend time watching trout run the same risks scientists rou-tinely run in trying to measure things without affecting them. Though I don't hesitate to call the trout I observed wild, I realize that Fishing Bridge itself, with its numerous pilings, shadows, and human travelers, introduced a massive artificial factor into their lives, not only with the generation of convenient currents they could ride, but also through its far-reaching effects on stream behavior downstream and its provision of a relatively predator-free environment. Ospreys and pelicans, though often bold in a protected natural area like Yellowstone, would be understandably shy in the presence of large crowds of tourists on the bridge and along the adja-cent shoreline. Other predators, such as otters and bears, would be much more shy than the birds. Fishing Bridge is a great and comfortable place to be a trout.

Local variations in environment aside, there has been an almost uni-versal conviction among angling writers that splashier rises indicate prey that are more likely to escape. This is one of the more or less trustworthy rules to come out of all the hours of watching done by these writers, but it does raise questions.

Trout, needing energy efficiency to survive, tend not to waste effort, and many writers have commented on the sedate and sometimes nearly undetectable rises of even large trout to spent mayfly spinners fatally trapped in the surface film. Many writers also have commented on the nearly frantic-seeming and splashy rises of trout to the many kinds of caddisflies whose emergence requires little or no time on the water's surface; it is even proposed that leaping fish are just continuing into the air the pursuit of caddis that they chased up the water column and continued to follow when the adult insect popped through the surface film and began to fly away. Clark and Goddard correlated the speed of the fish with the splashiness of the rise in this way:

> But wait! Does this not mean that there is not only a relationship between the speed of the trout and the speed of the creature it is pursuing, but a relationship, too, between the speed of the trout, and the violence with which the water is displaced?

> Yes, indeed.

The correlation of speed with the splashier rise has several intriguing elements. First, consider the small trout. Many of us have observed that small fish often make splashy rises to flies that their larger counterparts take with the quietest of sips. The assumption seems to be that small trout are simply less competent and rise with a puppyish exuberance that they will outgrow. We enjoy the thought that trout might experience adolescent awkwardness before achieving the calm of maturity. But much more is probably going on here than childish clumsiness.

Most important, the larger trout is far better able to generate the suction needed to pull a fly through the surface film and into its mouth. Achieving the same end is no doubt a greater struggle for the small trout, and the violence of its take may be the result of this.

Research by D. Weihs on suction-feeding hydrodynamics shows that a fish can significantly heighten the power and range of its suction by increasing its forward speed at the instant of the feeding episode. This, according to Weihs, helps explain the final burst of speed a fish may put on as it chases a minnow: That final little *umph* allows it to reach out and grab the minnow at a greater distance.

But this same process also may help account for the small trout's showy rise. If, for example, a small fish is compelled to go faster and suck harder in order to pull an insect into its mouth or even to drag the fly under, its speed and suction will certainly be evident in a splashier rise.

One would think, then, that the same thing should apply to any fish. The splashier takes we see so regularly when caddis are emerging seem likely to be the result of the fish going faster not merely to catch the insect, but also so it can reach farther and more effectively to pull the insect toward it. The violence of the surface rise under such circumstances is probably unavoidable, as the momentum generated by the acceleration often carries the fish higher out of the water. Indeed, if the fish is employing such heightened speed and suction to take fast-moving prey beneath the surface, the extended reach of its suction may even create surface disturbances that are misleadingly like actual rises.

There is a puzzle in the splashy rise that may be partly explained by this higher forward speed. Grasshoppers are famous for the explosive rises they inspire in feeding trout. And yet I have never seen or heard of a grasshopper that, once it has had the misfortune of landing in the water, actually managed to get itself airborne again.

Here are some questions about those grasshopper eaters. Don't trout notice after a while that these big creatures are no more able to escape than are the exhausted mayfly spinners that they so calmly suck down by the hundreds? Is the kicking and thrashing of the grasshopper enough to say, "I'm getting away," to the trout, and thus trigger the aggressive rise? Or does the grasshopper's larger size compel the trout to make a more assertive attack, create greater suction, and stir up such a mess of splash and splatter? Or is it some of both, or other factors as well, that cause the grasshopper to generate such dramatic rises?

Weihs also reported that there is a speed below which the fish's suction is not significantly improved, despite its forward motion. The fish still uses suction; it just doesn't need to enhance it. Some fishing writers have mistakenly assumed that only fast-moving fish bothered with suction, but in fact, even if the fish is moving slowly or simply holding in the current, the suction is as essential to its successful feeding. Eugene Connett III, in his generally very perceptive *My Friend the Trout* (1960), said that "should the insect be moving toward him in faster water, he merely opens his mouth and gills, thus permitting the water surrounding the insect to pass into his mouth freely, without the necessity of sucking it in." It would appear that there is almost always to one extent or another the necessity of sucking it in.

I say almost always because, like most rules, this one has exceptions. Aquatic nature lore contains numerous accounts of insect emergences that were nothing short of spectacular. Barnard Burks's *The Mayflies, or Ephemeroptera, of Illinois* (1953) reported on such an emergence in Illinois in 1940 that piled what the local newspaper referred to as "shadflies" to a depth of four feet on a Mississippi River bridge and required fifteen men with shovels and a bulldozer to "clear a path." These were probably mayflies, perhaps the famous *Hexagenia limbata* that midwestern anglers have imitated for many years. At such densities, the flies do not merely cover the water, but build up in thick mats on the surface. Such extraordinary quantities of food may allow trout to feed with little or no suction. In a recent conversation, British angling writer Robert Spaight told me that during his observations of trout feeding on phantom midges in a British stillwater, he saw fish "seining"—simply swimming along with their mouths open to capture large numbers of midges that were floating on the surface. Robert told me that when the midges reach these exceptionally high densities in the water, trout scooped up great numbers of them with no evident suction.

It's Up to Us

Comparing what so many experienced, perceptive anglers have written about reading the rise with my own experiences and photographic inquiries has not dampened my enthusiasm for the riseform at all. Though I agree with Clarke and Goddard that "the discovery of the principles behind movement and rise-forms, is about as close to the Philosopher's Stone that the fly-fisherman is likely (or, indeed, would want) to get," it appears that we are in fact on to something very important in this now-venerable little quest.

What I find encouraging throughout the literature of trout fishing is not so much the invention of Big Rules That Work Everywhere or a Unified Theory of the Rise as the great advantage to be gained through local observation. Again and again, it is quite clear that someone, famous or not, expert or not, has encountered a situation on this or that stream where fish behavior resulted in a riseform that had reliable, consistent meaning. The inspiration provided by Halford, Skues, Marinaro, and the rest is best directed not at reading everything they wrote, but at reading your own stream.

So I suspect, based on how few changes we've seen in the overall theory of the rise since Taverner's overenthusiastic list of sixteen was published in 1929, that it's not really up to the experts to improve on this study any more. Though I hope they'll keep at it, it's really up to each of us, on our own waters and in our own ways, to see what we can make of it. And I find that thought a great deal more exciting and satisfying than the idea that we should wait around for more experts to explain it all to us.

CHAPTER FOUR

Coping with Rejection

I f you've been fishing even a few years, you've watched a trout come up to your fly, give it a look, and turn away. That kind of rejection is discouraging, but at least it's a nice, simple message from the trout: "I don't like this." And at that point, you're welcome to apply whatever combination of stream savvy, folklore, and science you can muster—to try a different fly, a different tippet, a different presentation, a different prayer, or a different fish.

But there are other kinds of rejection that we could barely even recognize until recently. And whether we knew it or not, these other rejections often sent a more promising message: "That was very close; try again."

Anglers' deliberations on how trout take—or miss—a fly have constituted one of the quirkiest little narrative traditions in the literature of fly fishing. In his otherwise presciently insightful book *The Rod and Line* (1849), British angling writer Hewett Wheatley calmly explained that because of their somewhat underslung mouths, grayling could take flies from the surface of the stream only by turning upside down, doing a kind of backward loop-the-loop each time they fed. Imagine.

Not many years later, in 1878, a controversy raged for some weeks in the pages of *Forest and Stream* magazine over whether trout, conducting a similarly circular acrobatic maneuver, knocked flies into their mouths with their tails. One correspondent, the prominent New York angler George W. Van Siclen, reported that he routinely witnessed precisely this behavior on his local trout stream. So agitated were the angling community's commentators by such claims that several of the sport's biggest guns, including the famous fishing writers and fisheries authorities Charles Orvis, Reuben Wood, Seth Green, and Theodatus Garlick, weighed in with either pronouncements on why such a thing was silly or theories on what Van Siclen might have seen instead of what he thought he saw.

The problem with all such theorizing is the problem encountered by students of the rise already mentioned: The trout's take happens so fast that theorizing was all these people could do. As *Forest and Stream* editor Charles Hallock put it while moderating the tail-slapping debate, anyone who claims to have seen the take in such detail "must possess an electric quickness of vision."

Some people did in fact have a remarkably good eye for trout behavior. Others had an equally good intuitive sense of how trout actually do feed. But it wasn't until the past forty or so years, as scientists began applying the photographic technology that really gave us "an electric quickness of vision," that human observers have fully analyzed and appreciated the incredible subtlety of the trout's take.

What science has shown us is fascinating and perhaps revolutionary, but we fishermen are still catching up. Consider this: As recently as 1980, a respected fishing writer could say that to take a fly, the trout "simply opens its gill covers and its gills, lets the current flow through, and the hapless insect is trapped in its gills or throat. Of course, some fish pick a fly from the surface with a rapier-quick thrust or a vertical sipping rise, but these riseforms are more common with small insects or spent flies." This summary, though probably "common knowledge" among fishermen only twenty years ago, is now known to be so inaccurate as to compete with Wheatley's and Van Siclen's theories as fantasy biology.

The Hands of the Trout

Half a century ago, in his immensely practical book *How to Fish from Top to Bottom* (1955), fisheries manager Sid Gordon made a telling observation that probably stuck with lots of his readers:

> An angler should always remember that a fish has no hands. If he sees no enemy around, and something comes floating down with the current before his eyes, he seizes it with the only means in his power, his mouth. If it's food, he accepts it. If he judges it inedible, he shoots it out of his mouth as if it were jet propelled.

Gordon was right and wrong about the hands. Biologically, it's true that fish don't have them. But physiologically, they've come up with a really helpful substitute. It's odd that Gordon didn't seem to realize that his hands analogy could have been carried a little further. His remark about the fish's amazing ability to eject something from its mouth reveals some awareness of the natural valve system that makes up its head. In fact, the object *was* jet propelled.

Many scientific studies have examined suction feeding in fish. In the early 1980s, Johan van Leeuwen published a series of papers relating to this process in trout. In a study whose methods were as elegant as its analyses, he used high-speed motion-picture cameras to "map" the flow of fluid through the head of a feeding trout. If you are scientifically trained (physics of fluids would be especially helpful), you may enjoy reading the original publication. Besides learning to pronounce such charming words as *actinopterygian,* you become immersed in the fabulously complex world that exists in a trout's mouth, where rotational symmetries, vorticity distributions, leak currents, backwashes, maximal opercular abductions, and many other forces and wonders stir your imagination. But in mercy to most readers, I shall summarize just a few of his findings here.

The trout can exert an uncanny amount of control and precision in using suction. This is not just an indiscriminate vacuuming operation that sucks in whatever is nearby. As circumstances require, the trout can open or close its mouth at the right instant and to the right extent to tighten the focus of the suction, thus increasing both the intensity and reach of the pull. The fish often needs to do this, and it constantly makes many decisions about such things as it goes about its day. Suction is a very versatile tool.

The accompanying diagram portrays the general shape of the elongated column of water that is pulled into and through the trout's head in the process of feeding. The column's gradual increase in diameter and more abrupt decrease in diameter at its forward end indicate that the mouth opens more slowly than it closes. It is this rapid closing of the mouth that has led many writers to describe the fish as grabbing the fly as its mouth slams shut. In fact, the fly is already in the mouth, which closes rapidly to make sure it stays there. The suction already did the grabbing.

The diagram suggests the rough maximum distance at which a trout attempts to suck in prey. The target of the suction is usually less than a head length distant from the trout, which can wait until the insect is very close before pulling it in, especially when feeding in calm water. My photographs suggest that most of the time, the trout I was watching didn't engage the "tractor beam" to a significant degree until the flies were almost to their lips.

Precisely when the trout begins the suction is very hard to determine with casual photographs, however. Even with their mouths open only slightly, the trout I photographed could have been applying considerable

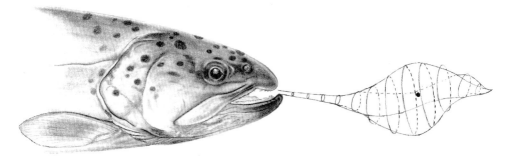

The trout's suction feeding typically pulls a double-tapered column of water into the mouth along with the prey. The suction column begins with a small diameter, as the mouth is barely open, and grows wider as the fish's mouth opens. The prey, signified by the dot in the center of the column at its greatest diameter, is usually within a head length of the fish before suction begins. The taper of the column is steeper beyond the prey; the mouth closes faster than it opens to ensure that the prey does not escape. By the means of this suction, trout routinely "reach out" to grab their prey. But the suction is sometimes defeated by artificial flies because of the resistance of leader and line. Illustration by Marsha Karle, adapted from a diagram in J. L. van Leeuwen (1984).

suction. And as I mentioned in chapter two, I suspect that a trout may also employ tiny jets of water in or out of its mouth to slightly manipulate and examine a potential prey item before applying its more forceful suction-feeding mechanism.

Trout have been using these "hands" for millions of years. Individual trout do it tens of thousands of times in their lives; they live by it practically from hatching until they die. They are, in short, experts.

Misses

Studying my photographs and then exploring the sizable technical literature on suction feeding sent me on an unsentimental journey back through the memories of more than thirty years of rises to my dry flies when the fish were not hooked—and because of my so-so fly-fishing skills, I have a very large personal database of such memories to evaluate. I recall myself saying again and again that comforting mantra of the fisherman who doesn't understand what just happened: "He missed it!" Or just as frequently, I would say, "He hit it!" or "He had it!"

But now, looking back with somewhat more educated eyes, I doubt all that. These fish are too good at what they do to have missed as often as I thought they did. As satisfying as it might have been to think the fly was missed because of the fish's incompetence, I just couldn't buy that anymore.

The scientific literature of predation contains many summaries of the success rate of various predators, and some of those are fairly low, especially in the case of a large mammal, which may have to engage in quite a few chases in order to bring down one prey animal that will feed it for several days. The stakes are high all around in cases like that. But the success rate of one predator tells us very little about the success rate of another, especially if their needs, prey, and methods are dramatically dissimilar.

Could all those trout I missed really have been that lousy at their jobs? Could they miss so often? Well, we do know a rising trout has some challenges to overcome. First, there's the trick of feeding on the surface of the water. Both Van Leeuwen's study and his diagram of the column of water that is sucked in by the trout are based on fish feeding under the surface.

My first interpretation of this photograph was that it showed a trout taking one fly while another slipped by. But I now suspect it shows a missed rise or, more likely, last-minute rejection. As the mayfly spinner passes over the trout's pectoral fin, judging from the angle of the trout's eye, the fish is watching the fly go—and perhaps considering another try at it.

I've seen no study that tries to model the much more complicated physics and geometry of that suction column as it passes from one medium (water) to another (air). So I cannot give you a corresponding diagram of the suction column as it applies to a trout's attempt to suck in a dry fly. But my photographs, inconclusive as they may be as diagrams of that passage of the suction from air to water, certainly show that much of the force of the suction is dissipated in pulling a broader disk of water down toward or into the fish's mouth. That magnitude of distortion of the fish's suction column would seem to greatly reduce the efficiency of the suction mechanism. This could make it a little harder to nail the prey, especially under otherwise marginal circumstances.

Thanks to a century of painstaking observation and analysis by the great dry-fly writers, we have learned that a fish taking a fly from the surface of the water is dealing with a complex set of visual variables that complicate its perception of any surface food it's trying to take. A rippled surface, the refraction of light as it passes from air to water, and all the other subtle wonders relating to what the trout sees that many of our greatest angling theorists have pondered no doubt increase the likelihood of a missed rise.

But for all those complications, the trout has had millions of years of evolutionary preparation for just this moment. And it's a veteran of thousands of similar feeding episodes in which it neatly sucked flies down from the surface of the stream. Even with floating prey, the trout is still an expert.

The scientific literature on predation is full of calculations of predation rates of various species. None always score, and some miss a lot more than they catch. Yellowstone's famous wolves, for example, successfully kill an elk in only about one of every five chases. If trout never missed, they would be the only animals that don't. But they're not cheetahs trying to run down gazelles; they're big fish sucking helpless little bugs off the surface of the water. They have too much going for them to miss very often.

So I realized it was likely that most of the time when I'd yelled, "He missed it," though I had indeed missed the trout, the trout probably hadn't missed the fly. Something else had occurred. The trout decided not to eat the fly at the last instant during the rise or took it and rejected it before I knew what happened. Or perhaps the fish never intended to take it and just came up for a splashy closer look.

Nature is very good at tuning up wild animals to do what they do and does this in a fairly brutal way. The most surefooted mountain goat may some day make that one fatal misstep it always seeks to avoid. But the odds are that before it does, it will have made several million competent, life-preserving, and entirely successful steps.

Despite all we have been taught about the reasons for trout selectivity, we are still surprised when trout reject our biggest and apparently most appetizing offerings of flies. There is some comfort in knowing that they also reject the real thing. This trout was feeding on much smaller insects and let this distinctively marked larger insect go right by without notice.

The same trout didn't approve of all the smaller flies either. In this instance, a mayfly spinner eased right along the middle of the trout's back. Even during periods of steady and apparently dedicated feeding on a given insect type, this and other trout I observed frequently rejected natural insects that, to me at least, seemed indistinguishable in species and life stage from the ones they ate.

Hits

Over the centuries, a long line of fishermen, most of them much more skilled at catching fish than I, have dealt with the harsher realities of the missed strike. Whole schools of thought have arisen about how to deal with "short strikers"—wait longer, wait less long, don't strike at all, strike harder, and so on. Other commentators advise us that it's not the timing of the strike so much as the direction. If, for example, you are fishing across the stream and a fish takes, you should set the hook by swinging the rod sideways rather than up, in a downstream direction, thus pulling the hook into the fish's jaw.

All this advice is good, depending on the circumstances. Similarly to learning to read riseforms on your local waters, the development of striking skills can be only partly taught. You have to experiment with what works best with your local circumstances and fish.

But striking will work only if the fish is indeed there to be struck. One of the revelations when learning about suction feeding is not so much that the trout is a sucker, but that maybe the angler is.

Francis Francis, the great all-around fishing writer of late-nineteenth-century England, used the apt term "pluck" to describe that little instant of resistance anglers often feel as a fly is either risen to, if it's a dry fly, or drifts along, if it's a wet. Others call it a hit, tap, or bump. We variously interpret this little bit of physical contact as a sign of a fish nearly taken, rejecting a fly, or in some other way directly interacting with the fly. Dave Whitlock has suggested that it could be caused by the fly dragging or bumping along the side of a trout that has just rejected it without the fisher knowing it. Whatever the pluck is, it's exciting but not an especially hopeful sign, because it seems to mean that the fish has felt the hook and probably won't come back again.

In 2003, shortly after my articles on how trout take a fly were published in *Fly Fisherman* and *Yellowstone Science,* I heard from Bob Bachman, one of the trout researchers who had been helping me sort my way through this subject. Bob is a biologist whose wonderful studies of brown trout feeding behavior in Spruce Creek, Pennsylvania, added so much to our understanding of what goes on in a trout population on a day-to-day basis. He had already, years before, arrived at an important insight on the matter of the pluck and how it connects with the suction feeding of trout.

> I was surprised that you didn't mention the observation that when fishing a traditional wet fly one often gets "short strikes". But they really aren't short strikes at all; the trout simply misses the fly because of the tension on the leader as it is dragging in the current. The tug the angler

feels is often the "suction," or perhaps the trout catching only the tail or bend of the fly, because the tension on the leader keeps the fly from being sucked fully into the fish's mouth.

The suction, in other words, is strong enough that we can feel it, like a tap, but it's not powerful enough to overcome a dragging fly. The leader and line, either because they were already pulling the fly through the current, creating drag, or just because their inertia prevented the fly from moving freely into the fish's mouth when the suction was applied, were too strong and resisted the suction. Even if your artificial fly weren't attached to a leader, its weight and mass would cause it to respond differently to the amount of suction that a trout might find sufficient to pull in a real mayfly of similar size. There are lots of variables to think about.

But the good news in all this is that your fly did not necessarily fail the trout's inspection. The trout may have tried to take your fly but did not feel it at all. Quoting from Vincent Marinaro's *In the Ring of the Rise,* in which he discusses missed strikes that were caused by untimely drag: "You have not frightened the trout, you have disappointed him! What you have done is to destroy his nice calculations and to take the fly away from his predetermined point of interception."

Having no understanding, or even awareness, of the leader, the trout doesn't know what went wrong with its normally successful feeding strategy. When you feel that tap, the odds are better than you might imagine that the trout did not feel the hook and is not spooked. So as Bob Bachman advised me, it's well worth going back to it with another, slightly slacker cast: "When I use the traditional wet fly technique, I purposely try to keep the fly in view and give slack just as the trout takes the fly. No short strikes that way (if I'm alert and quick enough)."

Many of the casting manuals contain excellent instructions for how to ensure an adequately long drag-free presentation. John Judy's book *Slack Line Strategies for Fly Fishing* (1994) provides an abundance of advice that is useful in correcting for this trout-disappointing moment and giving the fish ample opportunity to put its suction-feeding skills to work successfully. The tap is just the trout's way of saying, "Try again."

Spitting Out the Fly

My brother Steve, a precise and patient fly caster, recently related to me one of those dismaying yet educational moments we all experience that permanently affect our approach to fishing. This one pretty much caused him to give up on upstream nymph fishing because, he said, it convinced him there was no way he was going to sense the take, so why bother?

The extreme force with which the trout can expel a fly is revealed by the spurts of water escaping from this cutthroat's mouth as it concludes a successful rise. Note also the distortion of light caused by the rapid flushing of water from the right gill and the one-sided shadow indicating the extent of the flushed water.

I was standing on a bank of Armstrong Spring Creek with the sun behind me, looking down into a nice smooth run with several trout clearly visible, holding and intermittently turning, apparently to follow and/or eat some morsel in the drift (not on the surface). I tied on a smallish but visible-to-me nymph, cast it in at the top of the run, and watched it do a pretty good dead drift through the fish. During the drift, I observed fish suck in and immediately spit out the nymph. The intake/expel cycle was so instantaneous that I was unable, in good conscience, to even attempt a hook set; that is, my awareness of the rejection was essentially simultaneous with awareness of the take. (Maybe Ted Williams could do better?) Sometimes the same fish would repeatedly take in and expel my nymph on the same drift.

I have seen similar behavior in aquarium fish many times, where they repeatedly and rapidly suck in and expel a turd or other floatie that apparently approximates something they are used to eating.

I've heard similar stories from other fishermen, who were able to observe the amazing speed with which a trout can get rid of something it doesn't like. Unlike us, if a trout wants to spit something out, it doesn't have to roll it around and get it properly positioned on its tongue or work up enough spit for a nice, dramatic arc. The trout just reverses the forces that brought the fly in and expels it, as Sid Gordon said in *How to Fish from Top to Bottom* "as if it were jet propelled."

And there are an amazing number of reasons for rejection. In *Trout Biology* (1991), Bill Willers points out that trout may reject potential food because something about it doesn't look right, but they may also judge it by its odor and even by its taste. They can apply any of these senses with great swiftness and get rid of the object even faster.

So Who Hooked Whom?

The realization of just how effective and nearly instantaneous this process of ejection can be has made me reconsider not only the fish I've missed, but also the fish I've hooked.

As far as the fish I've missed, I now wonder how many more of those fish that I used to think missed the fly actually did take it but got rid of it so fast that I wasn't even aware of it. Part of the splash of the rise could easily

As a trout takes an artificial fly, its momentum continues to carry it forward. The trout may then move sideways, down, back, or a combination of those directions as it returns to its holding station. Almost any motion by the trout, even straight ahead, might thus serve to hook it, but our success in setting the hook depends on a combination of our own quick reflexes, the increased tension the trout places on the leader as it moves, and the trout holding the fly just long enough for those two forces to work.

have been the ejection of the water, air, and fly that the trout had sucked in just an instant before and then sent back out.

As far as the fish I've hooked, my respect for my reflexes and hook-setting ability has dropped a couple notches. I know that there are plenty of times when I did promptly set the hook and thereby secure a fish that otherwise could have eventually ejected the fly and gotten away. I've seen it happen quite clearly, and you probably have too. There are times when the fish's take and turn seem to happen almost in slow motion, and you just pull back on the rod with a nice, even strain. It has an almost textbook smoothness to it.

I also know that even with a fish that has grabbed the fly and is holding it, setting the hook once or twice is still a good idea, just to be sure that the hook's hold is secure. This has been my habit, especially with larger trout

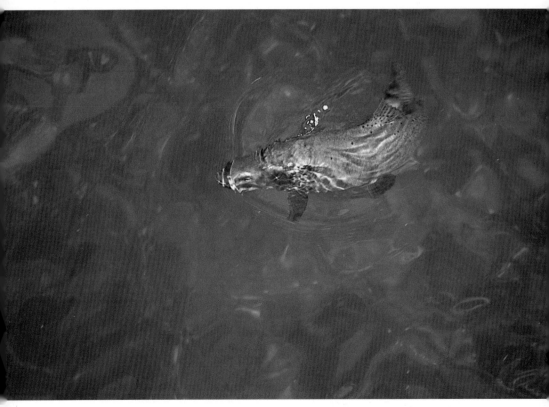

A faster and more violent take, especially if it involves a significant change in direction, seems more likely to cause the trout to hook itself even if the angler fails to set the hook.

on heavy tippets, when I can haul back pretty hard a few times just to settle the matter of whether I'm going to lose this fish right now rather than later. It's something Montana outfitter Richard Parks recommended to me many years ago, the first time I came into his shop babbling about having hooked and lost a big brown.

So I know that I can and do sometimes react well enough and fast enough to hook the fish myself. But I now assume that a considerably higher percentage of the fish that I thought I hooked actually hooked themselves, usually in the process of their posttake turn as they moved to resume whatever station they had occupied before rising. Among the infinite variations on this set of downward and lateral movements are a great many that cause the fly, with its movement-resistant line attached, to embed itself somewhere in the fish's mouth. If there weren't, we'd all catch a lot fewer fish.

The trout's attempt to take the fly is a finely tuned process, an act of predation that it repeats countless times in its life. It can't change the way it feeds. It's up to us to make sure that our fly, presentation, and knowledge are just as finely tuned to fully accommodate the predatory moment and give the trout every opportunity to successfully prey on our fly.

CHAPTER FIVE

The Trout's Field of View

I did not entitle this chapter "Trout Vision," because my concern here is considerably narrower than that. This book has little directly to do with all the mysteries involved in how trout see a fly. A number of fishing writers I've mentioned, including Harding, Marinaro, and Clarke and Goddard, have already covered the topic of trout vision in far greater detail than is necessary here. In addition, several recent scientific authors have written splendid popular summaries of trout vision. Judith Stolz and Judith Schnell's *Trout* (1991), Mark Sosin and John Clark's *Through the Fish's Eye: An Angler's Guide to Gamefish Behavior* (1973), Bill Willers's *Trout Biology: A Natural History of Trout and Salmon* (1991), Thomas Grubb's *The Mind of the Trout: A Cognitive Ecology for Biologists and Anglers* (2003), and Thomas Sholseth's *How Fish Work, Fish Biology and Angling* (2003) have kept anglers apprised of the latest thinking on how trout see.

I want to add just a few peripheral but perhaps helpful thoughts to this fine accumulation of information. In one or two respects, my observations and photography have altered my understanding of what trout can see, and in all cases these changes in my understanding have to do with the edges of the fish's visual range.

Of Windows and Mirrors

Many fishing writers have discussed the trout's "window," the circular portion of the water surface, directly above the fish, through which the trout can see beyond the water and into the terrestrial atmosphere. The window is formally known as the Snell circle.

The diagram shows how this works. The trout's view through the window is depicted as a cone, with its point at the fish's eye and its wide end constituting the window on the water surface. The angle of the cone is ninety-seven degrees, just a little more than a right angle, and it does not vary. Therefore, the deeper the fish is, the larger its window on the water surface. The closer it gets to the surface, the less widely it can see what is above the surface.

The evolutionary and survival trade-offs in these circumstances are pretty obvious. The closer the fish is to the surface, the more sharply it will see small objects on that surface. The deeper the fish is, the larger its field of view of objects on the surface but the less clear each object will be. The closer the fish is to the surface, the more effectively it may feed on surface foods but the more vulnerable it is to an airborne predator. Fish must constantly find the wisest depth, with the best combination of visual range, safety, and nutritional payoff.

It really is a window. Light striking the surface of the water within the fish's window passes through the surface. Light striking the surface outside the window is reflected, so the trout routinely sees the underside of the surface outside the window as a mirror or dark area. So do we.

The trout's "window" through the surface of the water is a circle, the high end of a ninety-seven-degree cone whose point is at the fish's eyes. Within this cone, the trout can see through the surface, though parallax causes visual displacement of objects above the water surface, especially toward the outer edges of the window. Beyond the window's edge, the underside of the water surface is mirrorlike. The trout detects approaching surface objects, such as floating insects, by the indentations, sparkles, and other disturbances they make in the undersurface mirror. ILLUSTRATION BY MARSHA KARLE.

But the angles are not simple, a fact well known among fly fishers at least since the time of Alfred Ronalds's *Fly-Fisher's Entomology* (1836). Refraction bends the light passing through the window, so the trout, as famously illustrated by Ronalds in his book, sees things that are in fact beyond the ninety-seven-degree angle of visibility prescribed by the cone.

The past century or so has witnessed numerous involved and technical discussions among angling experts over many aspects of the window. Especially great differences of opinion have arisen over what happens at the edge of the window, where an approaching dry fly first comes into the trout's view. (While outside the window, the trout is aware of the approaching dry fly because it either indents or protrudes in part through the mirror, creating what Clarke and Goddard poetically called a "starburst" pattern of light, which is the trout's first indication of an approaching insect.) Proponents and opponents of the importance of upright wings on dry flies have argued over just what it is the trout sees at the moment the fly reaches the window. Authoritative assertions on these matters are abundant and fascinating, for those interested in pursuing them.

Blind Spots

Though its vision beyond the surface of the water is thus limited to that one circular zone overhead, the trout otherwise has an extraordinarily large field of view. Like most animals at risk of predation, and like practically all animals that live in water and must potentially be aware of what's going on in any direction above, below, or around them, the trout has evolved with its eyes on the sides of its head. The trout's total field of vision is portrayed in the diagram. Each eye has a very nearly hemispheric view on one side of the trout. But much of the globular view that results is monocular, because only one eye or the other can see it. The trout has binocular vision, with the enhanced depth of field that accompanies it, only in a relatively narrow band that encircles the fish from front to back and top to bottom—that is to say, everywhere that both eyes can see. Binocular vision is no doubt of greatest help to the front, where the trout identifies and sizes up both prey and predators.

What has intrigued me for a long time about the trout's vision is the reported existence of the so-called blind spot, an area where, because of the conformation of the trout's head or limited ability of its eyes to move, it simply can't see anything. One of the first things to cause me to wonder about the blind spot was a somewhat mystifying comment in Vincent Marinaro's *In the Ring of the Rise*. Merely in passing, he mentioned that when a trout hovered at its usual inspection depth of about three

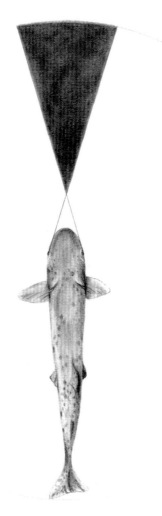

The trout has nearly a full circle of vision to its front, sides, and back. It can also see in all directions above it and much of what is below it. Most of this field of view is monocular, involving only one eye or the other. The trout's field of binocular vision is generally described as a narrow band in front of and above the fish, the primary areas that both eyes can see simultaneously. Most portrayals of the trout's field of forward binocular vision show it similarly to this. The dark triangular area approximates the full range of binocular vision. The smaller white triangle directly in front of the fish's snout is usually said to be a blind spot into which neither eye can see. Because of the placement of the trout's eyes far down on the sides of its head, some writers have proposed that this narrow triangular blind spot actually extends from the front of the trout up over its head, suggesting that it can't see directly above itself. My photographs indicate that this blind spot is very small, even when the trout is at rest.

CONTEXT

inches below the surface, a fly on the water surface right in the middle of the trout's window would be invisible to it because of "the blind spot above his head."

Other writers offered similar comments, all making the point that a trout's eyes are far enough down on the sides of its head that neither eye can see the space immediately centered in front of the mouth or above the head. Most writers only talk about the blind spot presumed to exist directly in front of the trout's mouth, but by implication the blind spot is believed to continue above and below the fish and broaden toward the tail, so that the trout is more or less encircled, especially near its skin, by an area it simply can't see. Note in the diagram the small triangle directly in front of the fish, an area into which presumably neither eye can see.

I don't doubt the possibility of the existence of this blind spot, or blind band, or whatever name we choose to give it. We can easily identify with the fish in this case. After all, only by making lunatic facial expressions can we see our own lips.

This limitation in the trout's vision, if it exists, is obviously no handicap to the trout. For one thing, no predator is going to be able to hide in that tiny little band of invisible water. For another, the trout's physiology is superbly tuned to get the job of feeding done. If the trout loses sight of its prey at the last instant, just before that prey enters its mouth, it matters little to the trout.

A Flexible Field of Vision

My photographs have convinced me, however, that in almost all directions we have overestimated the size of the blind spot and underestimated the trout's flexibility in getting a look at what it wants to see.

First consider the eyes themselves. The stereotype that has been passed down to us, based on "common knowledge" and the accumulated expertise of previous generations, is of a fish whose eyes are rigidly fixed in its skull, staring involuntarily outward. But in fact, the trout has an amazing ability to angle its eyes around—perhaps more so than we do. Gordon Byrnes, writing in *Fly Fisherman,* noted:

> Trout's eyes are located to provide an extensive peripheral field of vision. The cornea of the eye actually protrudes slightly from the side of the fish's head and renders it vulnerable to injury. The trout is able to move its eyes in a coordinated fashion by use of several muscles attached to the outside portion of each eye. By experimentally moving the eye with tweezers, scientists have demonstrated that the trout has a range of ocular motion comparable to that of the human eye.

Something has attracted the attention of this trout to its lower right. Note the extent to which the right eye has been bugged out and down and the equally impressive extent to which the left eye has been bugged forward, so that both are involved in watching whatever is of interest. Other photographs of this same fish show both eyes normally positioned. Its ragged upper lip may be the result of being repeatedly captured and released. This fish inhabited one of the busiest stretches of catch-and-release water on the Yellowstone River some miles downstream from Fishing Bridge. Catch-and-release fishing takes a wear-and-tear toll on fish that are caught again and again.

Even this accurate statement may understate the trout's capacity not only to turn the eyes this way and that in their sockets, but also to bulge them out in order to more or less "look around the corners" of its head. My photographs of trout with their eyes bugged out in various ways suggest the extent of this ability. When need be, the trout can probably eliminate almost all of the supposed blind spots in front of its mouth and above its head. This more complete range of vision is portrayed in the accompanying diagram.

A real trout is not a passive observer of its surroundings and does not function according to the limitations portrayed in the previous diagram. Scientific studies and my photographs indicate that a trout's eyes do not stare immovably out to the sides but are remarkably maneuverable. Thus even without moving its head horizontally or vertically, a trout can significantly expand the field of its binocular vision. It can, if need be, also virtually eliminate whatever minor blind spot might exist in front or above. In this drawing, the lighter-shaded areas on both sides of the dark triangle loosely approximate the extent to which the trout can enlarge the field of its binocular vision through its ability to redirect its eyes. In short, the limits of the trout's binocular vision do not hinder its feeding skills. If the trout requires a wider field of binocular vision than it routinely exercises, it can shift its head to a new position and aim the eyes to the best advantage. ILLUSTRATION BY MARSHA KARLE.

83

But the trout has even more going for it than its surprising ability to bug out its eyes in various directions. Because of the functional requirements of the mouth and gills, the head is somewhat flexible. When the gills flare, the mouth opens, or any combination of gill and mouth motions is being made, the eyes appear to be at least subtly redirected. As the mouth opens or the gills flare, the eyes are forcibly aimed more toward the front. I suspect that in this position, little is left in front of the trout's snout that does not fall into its field of view, whether the trout cares to see it or not. Combine that reshaping of the head with the trout's ability to bug out its eyeballs as it chooses, and the trout may have no more blind spot in front of or above it than an animal whose eyes are on the front of its face.

Perhaps the photograph that most impressed me with the trout's range of vision is the one taken from above and in front of the fish as it rose, showing the underside of the fish's jaw. The trout apparently was examining something, not visible in the photograph, that was under its chin. Though distance and the trout's motion made the image less clear than it might have been under more controlled circumstances, it is possible to

This trout is about to take a small stonefly. The slight distortion of its early suction is evident in the tiny flash of light between the shadows of the trout and the insect on the stream bottom. The eyes are aiming forward, as evidenced by the thin rim of whiteness around the back of the right eye.

The distinct rim of whiteness above the trout's right eye indicates the extent to which the eye is bugged. The left eye is bugged upward to look over the snout.

Though this photograph of a fast-moving fish was taken at too great a distance for the sharpness we expect in outdoor photography, it still shows that both eyes are trained downward to see a potential item of prey below the fish's jaw.

see that the trout is looking under its jaw with both eyes. In this case, the eyes are canted downward. I am unable to tell whether the head has been reshaped by gill or jaw movement or the entire effect was achieved by downwardly bugging the eyeballs. Whatever means the trout employed, my respect for its ability to expand its field of view is heightened further.

The Trout's Last Good Look

My photographs also suggest that there is not a disadvantage for the trout in trying to look up rather than straight ahead, but that its preferred angle of view for examining a closely approaching fly is a combination of the two.

We tend to think of the trout as coming toward the fly similarly to a bullet approaching a bull's-eye: The pointy end of the fish must be oriented directly toward the fly or the trajectory will be off and fish will miss the fly. According to this line of thinking, the fish is, in essence, leading with its mouth. The implication is that a trout approaches a fly by aiming its mouth, and thus its potential suction column, right at the

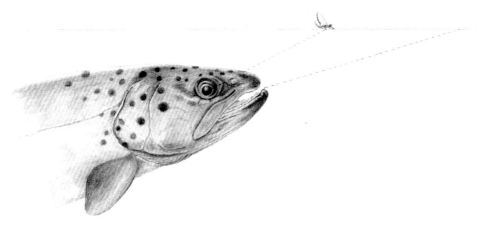

A rising trout traditionally has been portrayed like a bullet approaching a bull's-eye, with the pointy front of the fish moving directly at the floating insect. My photographs suggest that if a trout has sufficient leisure for a considered attack, it will instead approach the fly so that it can view it from slightly off-target, across the ridge of its snout. The trout may prefer this line of vision (the upper dotted line) for several reasons, including the ease of applying binocular vision at this angle or the fish's preference for holding horizontally in the current rather than at a head-up tilt. Only at the last moment, when the trout is fairly close to the fly, does it shift its trajectory upward slightly and lead with its mouth, along the course indicated by the lower dotted line. ILLUSTRATION BY MARSHA KARLE.

fly and closing in. The further implication is that the eyes are just along for the ride and must deal with whatever limitations in visibility such an approach entails.

But my photographs suggest that the process is more involved than that. In the first stage of the approach, especially if the trout feels the need to examine the fly carefully, the trajectory will be slightly off target, because the trout's preferred angle at which to examine the fly is not mouth-first. Instead, the approach brings the fish toward the fly so that it can examine the fly with both eyes, looking forward and slightly up across the bridge of its snout. The trout is not leading with its mouth, but with its best line of sight.

The drawing shows this stage of the approach as I have seen and photographed cutthroat trout performing it many times. Under the most favorable of feeding conditions, in a very slow, even current, the fish holds itself almost horizontal in the current, its tail perhaps slanting down a few degrees from level, and eases toward the fly. At this stage, the trout is not leading with its mouth. If you were to draw a line through the trout from the middle of the tail and out the mouth—the long axis of the trout's body—that line would pass below the fly.

Thus I assume that the trout's preferred binocular vision is across the bridge of the snout, perhaps halfway between the eyes and upper lip. My photographs suggest that not until the fish has approved the fly as prey does it make a slight shift of course, replacing its preferred line of sight with its preferred line of suction as its direction. From that point on, the fish leads with its mouth, moves forward, and sucks in the fly. This all happens so precisely, so smoothly, and with such practiced ease that the fish can hardly miss. And it happens so fast that we can hardly *not* miss seeing it.

Tilted Trout

Several writers in the previous century portrayed trout examining a floating fly, usually with the fish at an angle of forty-five degrees or more from the plane of the surface. Some of these older illustrations show the fish essentially vertical, with its tail pointing straight down, its head straight up, and the fly directly above the end of the fish's snout. Some suggest that trout routinely hold this position a long time, often drifting back under the fly as they examine it.

Such a posture is not impossible for a trout, and I've certainly seen them approach and take flies like that. But being upended so completely is a relatively inefficient position for a trout to maintain in a current; their entire body design works best when parallel to the flow.

Though when necessary a trout approaches a fly from any possible direction, it seems that when a trout has the luxury and leisure to approach the fly most carefully, the approach is much less acrobatic and does not involve tail standing. Given their druthers, the fish come in on a trajectory slightly beneath the path of the fly and keep a fairly even keel during the approach, though the tail does routinely seem to hang a little lower than the head, usually just a few degrees.

One reason a trout prefers this approach—besides its obvious energy efficiency in a current—is likely because it allows the fish the opportunity to best position itself to examine the fly in its preferred line of sight, looking up and forward across the bridge of the snout.

Right-Faced Trout?

Another intriguing observation of Vincent Marinaro's, from *In the Ring of the Rise,* is that "many trout feed only on one side of their face—that is, they take a fly from either the left or right on the drift. This leads to the speculation that trout may have a master eye and that they will position themselves where they can best see and then take a drifting insect."

I noticed no such behavior in my cutthroats, but that may be more a reflection on me or my trout than on Marinaro. There are too many potential variables between our observations for me to do more than speculate on his. The cutthroat trout I photographed seemed to range indiscriminately to either side to take flies. And they seemed, whenever possible, to line themselves up squarely as they drove in to take the fly and not to feed preferentially to either side. But I did not watch any individual among them long enough, or watch enough of them, to state for certain that none of them had a dominant eye.

It would make a fascinating study, requiring a demanding and carefully thought-out design, to determine whether some trout feed preferentially to one side. An individual fish doing so might have practical reasons, such as a damaged or less effective eye on one side, which would further complicate such a study. I haven't come across the notion of a master eye in the scientific literature on trout-feeding behavior, and I am not sure why such a thing would be to a fish's advantage, but that is not to say that Marinaro wasn't on to something. Trout will always surprise us. Surely that is one of the reasons we love them.

CHAPTER SIX

Are Trout Getting Smarter?

W e've all been there, and those of us who fish well-known waters have been there a hundred times. We arrive at a favorite fishing spot just in time to see someone leaving. Our chosen spot has just been fished. Maybe we move on, assuming they've put down the fish, but maybe we stay and give it a try, and maybe we even catch a few any-way—always good for the ego. And as we leave, someone else is pulling up or heading toward the pool from downstream. As we drive off, we casually wonder, "Don't these trout ever get any rest?"

But after a few years of seeing this sort of thing, we begin to wonder about bigger questions. Such as what this constant pressure—day after day, angler after angler casting so many flies, catching them again and again—does to the fish. If they're as savvy about survival as we claim they are, what are we doing to them with all this on-the-job training?

The education of trout is not a new story. The early books on trout-stream entomology—George Scotcher's *Fly Fisher's Legacy* (c. 1810), George Bainbridge's *Fly Fisher's Guide* (1816), and Alfred Ronalds's *Fly-Fisher's Ento-mology* (1836)—were all written because anglers needed to know trout-stream insects better in order to produce adequate imitations. Hard-fished trout were a reality in both British and American waters much more than a century ago, and when Ewen Tod, in *Wet-Fly Fishing Treated Methodically* (1903), said that "the more we fish, the more do trout become educated and knowing," he was not speaking to just a few anglers. Even in America, where the trout were supposed to be less experienced, the same idea was

89

often heard. For example, the August 8, 1888, issue of *Forest and Stream*, America's leading sporting periodical of the time, spoke of the difference between "uneducated fish" of lightly fished waters and those more wary trout on "well-whipped streams."

Today we all accept that trout get more difficult to catch when they're fished hard. Though the first few centuries of angling writing have little to say on this whole matter of trout getting smarter, for the past couple of centuries at least, angling theorists seem to have been driven to their great achievements by an unspoken urgency: Fish are getting harder and harder to catch, and if we don't keep cooking up new flies, lines, leaders, and other gear, they'll leave us behind completely.

Sure, the intensive commerce of modern fly fishing generates plenty of incentive for us to invent and buy new stuff. But it's pretty much agreed that the trout themselves really are demanding more of us as anglers. Today someone is always talking about the wise postgraduate trout of our hard-fished streams, and the ever-finer skills it takes to fool them, or the uneducated trout of our wilderness waters.

Did European anglers create a smarter or more wary brown trout by inadvertently culling the most catchable fish from each trout generation for many centuries? Thomas Bewick, the brilliant British master of woodcut engraving, published this scene of a trout being creeled, The Angler and the Little Fish, *in 1818.* HAND COLORED BY MARSHA KARLE.

The great irony of this process is that the harder the trout are to catch, the harder we work to come up with new techniques, flies, and other gear to catch them, thus continuing the education that Tod lamented a century ago. The circularity of the thing was pointed out by David Webster in *The Angler and the Loop-Rod* (1885) when he said, "Whatever leads to greater wariness on the part of the fish, will call for only a higher degree of skill on the part of the fisher." Webster thought this a good thing.

The great implication of the process is that through our intense fishing pressure, we have created a new and infinitely more discriminating trout population.

And the great question is whether this is really possible. Which leads to other questions: Did we truly reengineer the trout's brain in just a couple centuries? How in the world could we have done such a thing?

Brown Trout Puzzles

To address these startling notions, we must seek the answer somewhere over the long haul of history. Consider the brown trout, long known to be the most difficult species to catch. You might object to this talk of the difficulty of catching brown trout. Perhaps you have some personal experience that suggests that brown trout can be gullible. I have such experiences too, and I've heard others' stories. They're part of the lore of angling and are not only true but interesting.

In *Side-Lines, Side-Lights, and Reflections* (1932), G. E. M. Skues told an appalling tale of a brown trout that his brother hooked on four successive days, each day losing a fly. On the fifth day, he tied on a heavier tippet, again hooked the fish, and in attempting to horse it in, he tore away and retrieved only part of its upper jaw, festooned with all five flies. Skues followed that episode with an account of another brown, this one in Norway, that he and his brother hooked five times in the same day. Nobody said brown trout have National Science Foundation fellowships.

But a variety of scientific studies and the personal experience of many of us have shown that, on average, the brown is significantly harder to catch than the rainbow, brook, or cutthroat, just as those three in that order are progressively harder to catch than the others. The studies also suggest that though individuals of all these species might get harder to catch each time they've been caught, the brown trout gets harder fastest. This does indeed sound like a fish that is not only smarter, but also educable on a day-to-day basis.

So yes, brown trout do have "dumb days" when they are easily caught. So do the others. As well, on any given day, the other species might be uncatchable too. I've already mentioned how difficult brook trout can be under the right circumstances, and my occasional visit to Flat Creek in Jackson Hole, Wyoming, has given me the same respect for the Snake River cutthroat. But we're talking about averages here, and on average, the brown trout is significantly harder to catch than the others.

So the question remains: How did they get that way?

There's a theory that invokes the long European career of the brown as an angler's quarry, and it goes like this: If North American trout had, like the brown, been subjected to more than a millennium of steady and ever-more-sophisticated hook-and-line fishing the way the brown has, they might be harder to catch too. Century after century, generation after generation of smart fishermen all over Europe were in effect culling the easier-caught browns from the local populations. The trout left over in each generation were the ones that were demonstrably hardest to catch, and these were the ones that produced the next generation of trout, which was similarly culled. According to the theory, this slow process engineered a smarter trout through survival of the fittest—or in this case, the most cautious.

It is true that during this time North American trout also were being harvested by humans, but this was usually done with sturdier methods, such as spears, nets, and other devices that wouldn't necessarily encourage individual fish to develop fine discrimination about food choice (Europeans were also great masters of these early industrial harvesting techniques). The educated-brown-trout theory, then, concludes that purely by the accident of human cultural preference, with one species being stuck on a continent where lots of people used hooks and lines, the brown trout ended up the best prepared to deal with modern angling techniques.

I don't have the impression that there's a lot of agreement or even interest among biologists about this theory. After all, who's to say that the previous few million years of evolution didn't just make each of these species the way they are, independent of human actions? But the theory does have a pleasant plausibility. We know that things like this happen with animal populations sometimes, whether we do them on purpose or inadvertently. We know we can reshape the behavior of an animal without even taking it out of the wild. Look how quickly deer and grouse get warier when the guns start going off.

My friend Steve Herrero, one of the world's foremost bear biologists, told me about a small, isolated population of grizzlies living in the mountains of Italy. These bears have been subjected to enough centuries of incidental "training on how to survive around humans"—that is, getting killed when they mess up—that they have taken on all the behavioral traits of

In sharp contrast with what we know about the first nineteen or so centuries of fly fishing, modern anglers release most of the fish they catch. Though catch-and-release may not have the same dramatic effects on trout populations that traditional catch-and-kill practices did, catch-and-release fishing is a significant form of education for trout. Steve Schullery preparing to release a brown trout in Thompson Creek, Montana.

timid black bears, learning to be really wimpy and not eat anything humans want to eat. And good for them; they'd be gone if they hadn't adjusted.

Parent trout don't teach their young. Unlike the grizzly bear, which learns much of what it knows about life from a two- or three-year wilderness survival course taught by its mother, the baby trout is entirely at the mercy of instinct and experience. The theory that we can make a trout population smarter by killing off the dumb ones in each generation is pretty much the only way such a thing could happen, short of really long-term evolutionary processes. If we don't do it, who will? Certainly not the mother trout.

And I must admit, the theory is charming. It's kind of fun to think that we anglers, casting and casting and casting all those years, were actually involved in a kind of coevolutionary exercise with these fish. It makes them seem a little more connected to us—maybe not in the same league with the golden retriever, but certainly less remote than the rattlesnake.

Charley's Mystery

The above theory is tough to defend in its specifics, however. First there's this whole question of flies. There's been a lot of loose talk about trout getting to know specific fly patterns and therefore losing interest in them. Many anglers for many years have been sure we've seen particular fly patterns become less effective. Just a few decades ago here in the West, most effective fly patterns were huge attractors that would shock the modern techno-entomo-fluoro-angler—size 8 Humpies, cast-off Atlantic salmon patterns, oversize Catskill dry flies, nineteenth-century wet flies—and they were very successful. My friend Bud Lilly, who has fished through this entire changing era, tells me that though the Muddler Minnow was one of the staple big-fish patterns only forty years ago, he doesn't even carry one anymore.

But there's also a lot of talk about quicker changes in the tastes of trout, of flies that appear and fade in only a few years. "Trout get to know new fly patterns really fast," we hear.

I don't know. A trout's mental operations are so different from mine that it's hard to get inside its head, but even if the trout are mentally developing little personal field guides to our imitations, a lot of other things are happening too.

For one thing, some flies, such as the Elk Hair Caddis, to name a relatively recent pattern, and the Gold-Ribbed Hare's Ear, to name an older one, go on and on. Any experienced angler in my neighborhood could probably put together a pretty good list of fly patterns that keep working year after year. The fish never seem to learn that these patterns are fake.

Why would they not learn to recognize these along with the others? Are they just more perfect flies in some sense?

For another, commerce kicks in. We're slaves to fashion, and we're always looking for a better fly, line, or leader. The late and great outdoor writer Charley Waterman used to ponder the mysterious way fishing lures came and went, and a lot of that mystery had to do with a fickle market. A fly or lure is hot for good reasons, but also because we're susceptible to the marketing of hotness.

Commerce might have another effect, as pointed out by angling historian Ken Cameron, who has suggested that once a fly "has gone into commercial mass production, it is so changed that it no longer has any appeal." An excellent example of how commerce can change a pattern is the thorax dry flies originated by Vincent Marinaro. Marinaro's style of wrapping the hackle involved awkward angles that were a nuisance to tie, and the flies were not at all pretty by the standards of traditional styles. Almost without exception, the commercial versions are simply conventionally tied dry flies, but with the wing and hackle moved back toward the center of the hook and some additional body wrapped between the wing and eye. They still work, but they don't do justice to Marinaro's design.

Many of us have had the experience of trying out a new fly and catching a big batch of fish that first day. For most people, that's all it takes to abandon last week's favorite patterns. In many cases, the pattern may never do that well again. What happened? Was the fly less good after a while because the fish got to know it, or was its initial success a fluke? Think of all the patterns you've taken out and tried that didn't work that first time, so you gave them low grades and hardly ever tried them again.

Well, we won't solve Charley's mystery here. The acceptability of a fly pattern to trout seems to be an enormously complicated matter, and for all our heroic attempts at empiricism, I doubt that a panel of impartial, formally trained logicians would be much impressed by our pronouncements about the fading effectiveness of this or that pattern.

But let's look at it from the viewpoint of a trout population, because that is where we get into the most trouble.

Trout Populations

Thanks to a rich history of fisheries research, there's no question that fish can learn and apply such learning to prevent me from catching them. Whether they know that's precisely what they're doing is a different question; they're avoiding something presumably unpleasant that happened to them last time they behaved in a certain way, but that doesn't mean that they've reasoned out the sequence of events and consequences that would come from being caught.

A variety of studies with several species of sport fish demonstrate that fish can quickly become more discriminating in the face of fishing pressure. When they're caught, they do get harder to catch again. There is also adequate scientific evidence to prop up our frequent observations that trout become selective, ignoring other food sources in favor of one particularly abundant or otherwise preferable species of insect.

But these are all things that require only a few years in the life of a trout population. They don't require generations of anglers, and they don't require the passing on of certain behavioral traits from older trout to their offspring. If there are enough of us out there hammering the stream, we can do this to a trout population really quickly. It doesn't take decades.

Besides, remember the difference between the trout and the grizzly bear: The bear mother teaches her cubs, but nobody teaches the baby trout. They start fresh. Information the parents may have picked up during their lives is not transmitted to their offspring.

I recently posed some of these questions and issues to Dr. Robert Behnke, famed trout taxonomist-conservationist and author of *Trout and Salmon of North America* (2002). One of the most history-minded biologists I know, Bob has spent years rooting around in the various obscure writings on fish and fisheries management from the past few centuries. To him, the interesting idea that we have created a savvier brown trout through centuries of angling pressure could be possible, but it's not very likely: "I especially doubt a hereditary memory to avoid specific flies or lures has ever occurred." I agree.

Trout certainly seem to get harder to catch if they're fished heavily, but so what? We don't really know, over all those centuries, just what it was that the trout was learning to avoid. We've tended to assume it was most likely the fly or lure—something about its appearance or behavior, such as the visibility of the hook. Or maybe it was the leader or line. Maybe it was a human scent, the odor of the fly-tying materials. Maybe it was the angler's aftershave. There are just too many elements and variables in the situation, and there's too much we don't know. We're in the dark here.

But it's okay. We may have needed all those generations of earlier anglers to give us the technology and wisdom we now apply to our fishing, but the trout didn't need them in order to become so smart and uncatchable. The trout can make the change much quicker than that, especially if there are plenty of fishermen after them.

And as we all know and regret, there are more fishermen out there all the time, applying ever greater fishing pressure to their favorite public waters. A five-year-old trout that might have been caught every couple years in the 1920s or every year in the 1950s might be caught several times a season now. So the modern fish actually may be more educated in some sense than its counterparts in earlier generations. But it's not because it inherited its smarts from its ancestors. It's because we're causing it to learn more than those earlier generations of trout had to. There are more of us and probably fewer of the trout, and we're getting more and more technologically advanced and, presumably, knowledgeable about the trout's vulnerabilities. No wonder they're harder to catch.

According to Bob Behnke:

> The common belief that trout are more difficult to catch than in the old days, I attribute to this learning (nurture, not nature)—waters are fished much more intensely and by more skilled and experienced anglers than in the old days—and catch-and-release is much, much more common now, creating caught-and-shy, more wary trout. It's possible selection for wariness has occurred, but I doubt it has played much of a role.

Where this leads me is backward: Wouldn't it be fascinating, as well as a good way to test Bob Behnke's argument, to find some nice brown trout river somewhere and not fish it for, say, ten years just to see what would happen? I know, I know; every angler in America, even those who might agree with me that it would be an interesting experiment, would say, "Not in my backyard." But if we *were* to find such a place and could keep the fishermen off it for a decade (five years might do, but let's say ten just to be sure), we should have a truly wild, unmanipulated trout population. If it contained browns and rainbows, would we still find the browns to be much "smarter" than the rainbows? Surely after ten years, the fish would have reverted, as much as possible, back to their naive state. How much easier would the browns be? Would the rainbows be as easy as cutthroats? What would all that free time without us pestering them do to the famously hard-earned, Ph.D. grade selectivity we have taken for granted as the way of these trout? And if they were a lot easier to catch, would we end up liking them less because they were so dumbed down? In short, how important is it to us that these fish be hard to catch?

For many of us, the difficulty of catching trout is not just a product of our long angling history, but a requirement of it. Many of us lose interest in fishing for trout that are too easy to catch. For many, backcountry fishing for truly wild trout is a novelty, not a staple. We need more from the fish, and the only fish we can get it from are the ones we've made that way. This leads us back to the notion that we and the trout have been engaged

The progressively more difficult challenges of hard-fished trout waters have created a school of anglers for whom such fishing is essential to the game. Our sport thus depends not only on the trout, but also on the collective and cumulative effect of many anglers on many trout. Ed Koch on Letort Spring Run, Pennsylvania.

in something together—if not evolutionary, it seems that at least we've participated together in a many-centuries-long partnership of sorts, a kind of skill-building competition.

We have spent a couple thousand years, maybe more, going at it with these fish, a long, slow, stumbling advancement toward something we like to think of as enlightenment as we reshaped the fish. Like the lynx and snowshoe hare of the Far North, anglers and trout have shared the ages in a kind of competitive tension for so long that it would be hard for us to simply withdraw from it now. We have defined our sport for so long in terms of the trout's talents for eluding us that the whole enterprise might just fall apart if suddenly the rules were changed and the trout got easy again.

There are other interesting definitions here, including the very idea of wild trout. Trout in special-regulations waters are often caught again and again. Some years ago, a study in the Yellowstone River catch-and-release water in the park indicated that the adult cutthroat trout in that water were caught an average of 9.7 times each, every summer. Some were caught two or three times a day, an experience with them I've had myself. Whatever questions that study may raise about the trout, it raises even more about the anglers. A trout can get pretty ragged after being caught and released so often. Several of the fish I photographed looked pretty beat up in this respect. There are, or should be, aesthetic issues here, assuming that we've come to terms with the moral issues that make so many of our critics uneasy or angry about catch-and-release.

How much of the training that we give these trout is good, and does it ever reach a point that it's destructive to the fishing experience, not in terms of the fish becoming uncatchable, but in terms of the fish being caught too often? How often can a wild trout be caught and released and still be wild? When does it become so accustomed to the experience that its behavior, our clearest evidence of its wildness, is affected and it becomes in some sense domesticated? And what about our view of what happens when we catch that fish? Do the previous catchers matter? Is the twentieth person to catch it having the same experience as the first? Is this exhaustive repetitive use of trout the best approach we have to look forward to in the future of trout fishing? Or will we eventually decide that so much recycling of the same experience unacceptably reduces its authenticity?

Apparently most of us still think things are going okay in today's catch-and-catch-again world. We aren't paying much attention to questions like these yet, but some day I think we will. Fishing involves a good many compromises and concessions to necessity, and it takes us a while to decide which ones are tolerable.

For a helpful overview of what is scientifically known about learning and memory in trout, see Thomas Grubb's 2003 book *The Mind of the Trout.*

First Base

In my book *Royal Coachman* (1998), I made a comparison or two between fishing and baseball, and another one occurs to me here. It has been said about baseball that despite all the things that the psychopathically greedy people who run major-league baseball do to tinker with the rules, equipment, playing fields, and players' physiology, it continues to work because the fundamentals endure. It is still true, as one sports writer has put it, that after upward of two hundred years, a smartly hit grounder,

Anglers and managers, having labored for generations to ensure the survival of many trout populations, haven't yet had the luxury to explore the philosophical complications of fishing for trout that have been caught and released many times. Are a trout's inherent wildness and the fisherman's experience in some way compromised by repeated catching of the same fish? I caught this relatively wild trout in the Yellowstone backcountry. PHOTOGRAPH BY MARK JOHNSON.

fielded competently and thrown accurately by the infielder, will beat even the quickest runner to first base by a step or two. As the average player's physical skills improve, they tend to do so apace with all the other players; the faster pitcher throws to a quicker batter, and the stronger batter hits to a fleeter outfielder. It's not a perfect system. It wobbles nervously along, and we tend to nudge it out of kilter sometimes, but it's so fundamentally sound that it keeps working. The basic institution has thus proven its genius.

It is, similarly, one of the serendipitous wonders of fly fishing that, for all our improving technology and heightened understanding of trout, we still meet these fish on roughly the same one-on-one terms as did our ancestors hundreds of years ago. This is not to say the sport hasn't changed. It has changed in many ways, and most of us even think it is better than it was.

Certainly it's changed with finer technology. Our faster fly rods may enable us to set the hook a little quicker, and perhaps we've gained a millisecond edge. But they also enable us to fish considerably farther off, and the intervening length of line, even as fancied up as it has been by modern industry, must absorb the greater stretch and shock of the strike to set the hook at a greater distance.

In our engagements with the trout, the advantage, if that's what it can be called, seesaws back and forth. The harder we fish for trout, the harder they become to fish for. No matter how smart we get, they still seem smart enough to elude us most of the time. Nature still presents us with variables beyond counting. The entire enterprise is still blessed with glorious unpredictability. There are still days when it's all easy and days when it's all impossible. In so many ways, no matter what we do to heighten our skills and improve our tools, the trout are still the experts.

After a recent presentation of my photographs of rising trout, a woman in the audience objected that this sort of study took too much of the mystery from fishing, that I could be ruining the sport for myself—and, I think she implied, others—by dissecting the trout's rise so thoroughly. I happily disagreed, saying that what I'd learned just made it all the more exciting and didn't seem to reduce the mystery at all. Some people in the audience were bold enough to agree with me.

The mystery of fly-fishing for trout doesn't lie in any physical process or behavioral instant. It lies in the amazing way it all fits together and sustains its fascination. It lies in the endless choices we make about how we want to participate in the trout's world. It lies, at heart, in the beauty we find in that world and its workings, and beauty is always the best kind of mystery.

PART TWO

How We Take a Fly

*But flytiers since the beginning of time have been looking for flies
that the fish will find irresistible under certain conditions,
if not all conditions. It seems a worthy search, however irrational.*

RODERICK L. HAIG-BROWN, *A PRIMER OF FLY FISHING* (1964)

CHAPTER SEVEN

Tradition and Revolution

Most people who have been involved in fly fishing for more than thirty years would probably agree that the sport has undergone a transformation in that time. It has changed at a pace never before experienced. It's easy enough to point to some symbols of these big changes. Consider, for example, a few books.

Lefty Kreh's terrifically graphic book on fly casting opened our eyes to a whole new "right" way to cast, and I'm sure that I'm only one of many who, whether we adopted all of Lefty's recommendations, were quick to incorporate this or that part of his style into our own approach. Besides, some of us, never too hot at the more upright old casting style anyway, felt relieved to suddenly discover that our undisciplined low backcasts were now okay, maybe even cool.

Charlie Brooks's heavily weighted nymphs offered a successful challenge to a several-centuries-old aesthetic stance in which flies were necessarily weightless. Charlie's books were certainly a key part of my awakening to the full range of fly patterns available to a western angler.

And probably the most far-reaching of all American fly-fishing books since World War II, Doug Swisher and Carl Richards's *Selective Trout* (1971) elevated our thinking not only in fly-tying theory, but also, through its wonderful photographs of insects, in our basic understanding of what the flies really imitated. Additionally, it inspired generations of new amateur entomologists and no doubt had other secondary effects we are not aware of.

The arrival of the graphite fly rod on the market also makes a good marker for the beginning of the modern fly-fishing revolution, and I imagine you may have other milestones in mind. Altogether, the changes were remarkable. The average modern American fly fisher even learns to fish differently than did earlier generations. After several centuries during which most anglers were taught to fish by relatives or friends, the process was homogenized and professionalized by the post-1970 flood of new books, magazines, videos, and now websites; the proliferation of fly-fishing clubs and conventions; and the establishment of several good fishing schools. Within a very short period of time, we went from learning primarily local knowledge slowly over the course of a fishing life to having immediate access to everything that everybody knows everywhere.

All this has happened with enormous fanfare and more than a little self-congratulation. Leading anglers, magazines, and a wide variety of commercial enterprises constantly remind us of how innovative we have become and—this implication is overwhelmingly clear—how proud we should be of ourselves and our new open-mindedness.

Well, maybe. There are still some doubts out there whether we're better off for all the new toys and tactics. But the rate of change has been unprecedented in the history of the sport. It has been one of those rare periods when an institution experiences a genuine revolution.

Tensions

I feel especially fortunate that my involvement with fly fishing has spanned the period since the publication of *Selective Trout*. In fact, when Swisher and Richards brought out a new, revised edition of the book in 2000, beautifully illustrated by Dave Whitlock, who just keeps getting better, I considered it a distinct honor that the publisher quoted me on the jacket. It's nice to become a part, even in such a tiny way, of something that has meant so much to the sport's modern revolution.

And yet fly fishing still leans hard on its traditions. One of the most charming things about fly fishing is that not only do we use many techniques and hold to many values that were developed long ago, but we also know and honor the names of the people who gave them to us. In the great binge of angling innovation over the last three decades, many of us may have lost actual sight of that tradition, but what with the appearance of several fly-fishing museums, a number of fine specialized periodicals, and a lot of books, the tradition is in the hands of good keepers and isn't going to vanish. It will be there waiting for the attention of any newcomer who chooses to look deeper into the sport.

The longer I fish and the more I read the older writers and study the sport's history, the more I see fly fishing as a huge, multigenerational con-

Angling tradition is more than the accumulation of centuries of technique, lore, and wisdom. It is the highly personalized way by which those things are passed along from generation to generation. It is the combined impact on the sport of each generation as it learns the sport and makes it its own. Steve Schullery and his son Dan tying a fly.

versation. Our best fishing writers, even hundreds of years ago, conducted their instruction that way, pausing here and there to inquire into the sense of some earlier writer's theories or recognize another for an idea clearly realized. To give only a few of several excellent modern examples, take a look at Alvin Grove's *Lure and Lore of Fly Fishing* (1951), Gary Borger's *Nymphing: A Basic Book* (1979), or Datus Proper's *What the Trout Said* (1982). All are important original works that also pay congenial respects to their many predecessors. It's easy enough to just intone the names of the greats, but it's quite another to take up their questions and see where the inquiry leads.

It's rare that anything wholly new comes up in this process, but often the conversation does add new information or insights to what already is there. And a lot of the time the conversation is heated, even quarrelsome. This is the product of what fishing historian John McDonald, in *Quill Gordon* (1972), called "the tension between classicism and innovation," which, as he pointed out, is itself not new but an enduring part of the sport.

It's how fly fishing works. Someone pronounces a Great Angling Truth, and if others notice and agree, it becomes ensconced in the code many of us tend to follow. Then someone else comes along and turns the whole

107

thing on its head. For every Halford, there will be a Skues. People get upset, other people get excited, others ignore the whole thing and go their own way. Maybe we all learn something, maybe not, but on we go.

That is the fly-fishing conversation at its best. It is illuminating and entertaining far more often than it is decisive. So many people are talking at once, with more voices joining in with each generation, that it's hard sometimes to make sense of it. But when all else fails, the delicious tension between the old and the new will always guarantee that a lot of engaging talk goes on.

Blends

In *Fishing from the Earliest Times* (1921), one of the few bona fide works of serious scholarship about angling history, historian William Radcliffe combined whimsy and wisdom in his assessment of how anglers think. Notice how nearly he agrees with Aldo Leopold, whom I quoted in my Preface, when he says, "The psychology of the faithful is an odd blend of dogged, perhaps unconscious, adherence to the olden ways and of an almost Athenian curiosity about 'any new thing,' which as often as not sees itself discarded in favour of the ancient devices."

In tracing our changing perceptions of the trout's rise in part 1 of this book, I suspect that I exposed a fair amount of that whimsy and, I trust, quite a lot of wisdom among all those sincere souls who for centuries have tried to put us on the right track in understanding these subtle and enchanting creatures.

In part 2, I propose another tour of those same centuries, this time to consider and enjoy some helpful examples of how fly fishing reflects Radcliffe's "odd blend" of tradition and innovation in its wonderful, slow accumulation of ideas and methods. We seem to have accelerated that accumulation in recent years, if only by seeking out ever finer modifications and permutations of the old ways. But the process has been with us for a long, long time.

Fly fishing was not initially constructed in any one person's mind or in any one person's book. It is a dynamic and energetic thing, the product of a host of intellects ranging from the brilliant to the daffy. The line between the two extremes is not always clear. And even when it is, sometimes we find the daffy more attractive anyway.

CHAPTER EIGHT

Deep Basics

I would be interested in learning about fishing history even if it didn't make me a better fisherman, but it has. It has because the long view—the generous sweep of history—rarely fails to reveal the continuity of good ideas and the accumulation of careful observation. History sorts out the silly, highlights the durable, and honors the brilliant—and if you happen to enjoy the silly, history will acquaint you with it at its best. I'm still learning from the oldest fly-fishing writing we have.

But I have to overcome a lot of prejudice to do it. As Radcliffe, McDonald, and others have pointed out, we fishermen get pretty set in our ways and pretty sure of ourselves.

Consider John Waller Hills's congenial *History of Fly Fishing for Trout* (1921), a recognized "classic" angling book if ever there was one. Hills started his chronicle of fly-fishing history by evoking a misty and irrelevant past. He pointed out, rather condescendingly I thought, that in the second century A.D., a "Roman author" left "an account of fly fishing for a fish, apparently a trout, in a river in Macedonia." The name of the author, Claudius Ælianus, whom we now familiarly call Aelian, was even relegated to a footnote. Hills dismissed this seminal fly-fishing episode as meaningless to us today because it had no connection to "the true history of fly fishing," which, according to Hills, began with the publication of the British *Treatyse of Fishing with an Angle* in 1496.

Hills, a man of his time, epitomized the sport's snootiest tradition, the very essence of white angling supremacy. For him—and he makes no apologics for this view—the entire history of the sport was aimed by fate,

109

and probably by God as well, toward the development of the dry fly, all so privileged types precisely like Hills could celebrate their own perfection by casting on the world's most expensive and exclusive trout streams. As a world view, it was quite tidy and no doubt enormously comfortable.

What entertains me about Hills's approach is that he found it so easy to say that though we fly fishers have a known history of about eighteen hundred years, the first thirteen hundred years didn't matter. Luckily, a lot of people have taken a more penetrating view. Within the past thirty years or so, many writers, mostly in England and Europe, have gone back to Aelian's brief account. They've theorized about not only what river Aelian's angler might have been fishing, but also what the fish species was, what insect was being imitated, and what the imitation looked like. There's no consensus on the river, but it's agreed that the fish was most likely a trout. As far as the insect and the imitation, we just don't know, but some of us would like to think we do. Some people have risked life and limb traveling through a lot of unfamiliar and even hostile country trying to figure all this out. That alone might make us wonder if Aelian is worth paying attention to.

The Original

So let's listen to Aelian for a minute. I'm quoting from what I am told is "the authoritative modern edition" of his *On the Characteristics of Animals,* translated by A. F. Schofield (1958–59).

> I have heard and can tell of a way of catching fish in Macedonia, and it is this. Between Beroea and Thessalonica there flows a river called the Astreaus. Now there are in it fishes of a speckled hue, but what the natives call them, it is better to enquire of the Macedonians. Now these fish feed upon the flies of the country which flit about the river and which are quite unlike flies elsewhere.

He then devoted a couple hundred words to the natural history of the insect, how the fish feed on it, and how unsuitable such a fragile insect was as bait:

> They do not look like wasps, nor could one fairly describe this creature as comparable in shape with what are called Anthedones (bumblebees), nor even with actual honey-bees, although they possess a distinctive feature of each of the aforesaid insects. Thus, they have the audacity of the fly; you might say they are the size of a bumble-bee, but their colour imitates that of a wasp, and they buzz like a honey-bee. All the natives call them Hippurus. These flies settle on the stream and seek the food that they like; they cannot however escape the observation of the fishes that swim below. So when a fish observes a Hippurus on the

110

Modern fly fishers have a very long reach. Only money stands between them and the world's most remote rivers. Only a little casting practice stands between them and that tempting pool along the far bank. And only some easy reading stands between them and a wealth of ecological information about the trout's world. And yet for all those advantages, it would be naive for us to declare that fly fishing is necessarily a better sport now than it was for our ancestors. Gary Tanner on the Firehole River, Yellowstone Park.

surface it swims up noiselessly under water for fear of disturbing the surface and to avoid scaring its prey. Then when close at hand in the fly's shadow it opens its jaws and swallows the fly, just as a wolf snatches a sheep from the flock, or as an eagle seizes a goose from the farmyard. Having done this it plunges beneath the ripple. Now although fishermen know of these happenings, they do not in fact make any use of these flies as baits for fish, because if the human hand touches them it destroys the natural bloom; their wings wither and the fish refuse to eat them, and for that reason will not go near them, because by some mysterious instinct they detest flies that have been caught.

He then explained that the local fishermen solved this problem by tying a fly, but let's be careful about our presumptions here. It has been pointed out by students of this episode that Aelian never actually said that the fishermen were tying their artificial to imitate the actual insect he had just described. This is what Aelian said they did:

111

And so with the skill of anglers the men circumvent the fish by the following artful contrivance. They wrap the hook in scarlet wool, and to the hook they attach two feathers that grow beneath a cock's wattles and are the colour of wax. The fishing rod is six feet long and so is the line. So they let down this lure, and the fish attracted and excited by the colour, comes to meet it, and fancying from the beauty of the sight that he is going to have a wonderful banquet, opens wide his mouth, is entangled with the hook, and gains a bitter feast, for he is caught.

Eighty years ago, when Hills dismissed this story as trivial, it was probably easy enough to agree with him that it was "interesting rather than important." But as more and more smart people studied it, as well as European angling history generally, it started to sound a little more important.

Locals

Two of these new researchers, medieval scholars Willy Braekman and Richard Hoffmann, came to my attention about twenty years ago. The two men, especially Hoffmann, a professor of history at York University in Toronto, have published a number of previously unknown early documents on fly fishing written prior to the time of the *Treatyse*. Hoffmann's numerous articles and one remarkable book have done more to reshape and clarify our understanding of the origins of fly fishing than the work of any other writer, ever.

The effect of having a real historian's take on fishing history was profound. Hills was not only wrong in announcing that the *Treatyse* was the beginning, he was *way* wrong. It soon became clear that local fly-fishing traditions had been scattered around Europe centuries earlier. North-central Europeans were fond of the *vederangel* (feathered hook) at least as early as 1200 A.D., and the documentation did not suggest that such usage was new even then. The documentary trail gets fainter as it gets older, but Hoffmann's work reduced a 1,300-year blank space in fly-fishing history to 1,000 years and gave some of us reason to assume that it could be reduced further as research continued.

Meanwhile, other writers reminded us of the survival of traditional fly-fishing practice in various isolated regions around Europe. These traditions involved noticeably Aelianesque tackle: rods with no reels, short lines, and straightforward hackled wet flies of the most utilitarian design. They also were carried on by people with no particular interest in the literary end of the sport—people unlikely to leave a written record of their fishing.

Angling historians began to put these local stories together with what was already known. We already knew, for example, that in 1897, G. E. M.

Skues, who later became one of the twentieth century's most influential angling writers, visited Bosnia, where he was outfished by locals using just such minimal gear. They had longer rods and lines and four-fly casts, but the basics of their presentation must have been about the same as that angler described by Aelian. These fellows hadn't learned to fish from the British or from outdoor magazines. They had inherited their approach from countless previous generations of locals just like them.

Other, similarly local fly fishers have gradually come to our attention. In northwestern Italy, a style of this fishing known as *Alla Valsesiana* employed similarly uncomplicated gear—again with longer rods but still without reels—and dated back beyond local memory. Other local practices are known to have thrived, either well into the twentieth century or even until now, in Serbia and Spain. The best summary of these pockets of local fishing tradition is in Andrew Herd's *The Fly* (2001). I imagine there were, and maybe still are, others.

I enjoyed watching historian Hoffmann whittle a few centuries off the front end of gap between the *Treatyse* and Aelian. But it wasn't until I'd read some of these other writers—the chaps who were tiptoeing among the land mines of Eastern Europe trying to rediscover ancient drainages and obscure regional fishing techniques—that it suddenly dawned on me what was happening here. Whether they meant to or not, *these guys were erasing the entire gap*. Even without locating actual documentation of people fishing in each century between 200 and 1200 A.D., they were offering a plausible scenario for how fly fishing had survived, mostly through local practice, mostly at the hands of illiterates who might have fished for both subsistence and fun, and entirely without leaving an obvious trace.

It's a terribly satisfying scenario. For at least two-thirds of the past eighteen hundred years, fly fishing thrived without all the social trappings and status that now surround it. It survived without tackle companies, international celebrities, books and magazines, ESPN, or history nerds like me rooting around in its traditions trying to understand where we came from. Fly fishing didn't need literary celebration. It was just something people did.

Local Experts

Best of all, it worked really well. It had to, or most of these people wouldn't have had time to fool with it. The writers who have been exploring all this history have urged us not to see these unnamed and unheralded fly fishers as rustics or primitives. They knew their rivers by living on them; they knew their tackle because they relied on it. They could outfish a young

G. E. M. Skues in 1897, perhaps inspiring him to tie his first nymphs in the process, and I'll bet their ancestors a thousand years ago could have too.

Talk about a lost saga. Imagine how many of these anglers, on how many rivers, made wonderful discoveries, accumulated lifetimes of wisdom to pass on to their children, and had richer lives for the rivers they fished. No doubt much of this happened in the brutal social and political environment the so-called Dark Ages are still famous for, but maybe the river lightened the mood of all that misery a little now and then.

Imagine as well all the lost learning in such a localized set of traditions. Here in one drainage, a few generations of anglers may have put together just the right combination of ingredients for the best flies and techniques possible. But unsupported and unencumbered by any written record, the craft was easily lost or set back. As Andrew Herd put it, "Who knows what knowledge was painfully gained, only to be snatched away by plague, war or famine?" Who knows, besides that, how many times such knowledge was lost and regained?

On the other hand, who knows what knowledge did get recorded by some literate member of this early angling fraternity, some casual observer, or some other forgotten Aelian? Even the compiler of the information in the *Treatyse* credited much of its instruction to earlier books, and those books, if they were not just an affectation invoking pretend authority to heighten the *Treatyse*'s own, may have had their own written sources. Our homework isn't done.

The success of these traditional fly fishers has made me think more about how I fish. Several descriptions of their descendants, fishing in the past century or so, celebrate the extreme efficiency and deadliness of short, quick casts and brief drifts through the pocket water of small mountain streams. Because this was a game played up close. They didn't reach out; they crept up. They never saw or heard of, much less owned, a reel. They dealt in pinpoint short-range sweeps of their flies through pools they knew exactly how to fish because they had fished them their whole lives. So had their grandfathers. They played every angle, exploited every bit of cover, struck at the slightest bulge or flash. They fished their horsehair line and small, unweighted flies on top or very near the top—so close that they may have had the fly in sight about as much of the time as a modern dry-fly fisherman does.

That all sounds good to me. I have spent much of my fishing life in places just like that. As impressed as I have been by fishermen I know who make heroically long, elegant casts, I have been even more impressed by the ones who eased up so close to the fish that all they cast was the leader. The past couple summers, under the influence of Aelian and his heirs,

Disciplined by necessity and the simplicity of their tackle, fly fishers from Aelian's time until well into the 1800s did all their fishing within two rod lengths' distance. Few anglers traveled far from home, so combining an intensive lifelong experience on local waters with the streamcraft and stealth required for success at such close quarters must have bred an amazing familiarity with the neighborhood trout. Thomas Bewick engraved this scene of an angler working close in a small pool below a riffle in 1804. HAND COLORED BY MARSHA KARLE.

these lessons have soaked in all over again, and I find myself eyeing each rock and pool from a different angle than I did before. I'm fishing leaders more than I ever did before.

Ancient Masters

Thanks to all this new information, I also think about the origins of the sport differently. I don't assume that just because Aelian told us about some fly fisher in Macedonia eighteen hundred years ago that this must be where and when it started. Actually, I don't assume it started in any one place, and as far as Macedonia goes, it wouldn't surprise me at all if fly fishing already was an ancient practice there when Aelian heard about it. These days, the mood among the European fly-fishing historians is that the sport most likely found its way to England from these older angling communities, and I enjoy the reversal of stature this delivers to Hills's snooty view of himself as the heir of a purely British invention. It's obviously a much more involved story than that.

In fact, I've wondered for some time now whether fly fishing isn't such an intuitively sensible practice that it might have started—and winked out and started again—many places over the centuries. Once hooks were readily made, why not? After all, Andrew Herd pointed out in *The Fly* that "anecdotal evidence makes it seem probable that fly fishing was known in Japan as early as the late eighth and ninth centuries B.C." Who's to say it wouldn't have been invented again and again, flourishing here and there wherever fish rise, until it finally fell into the hands of literate people who claimed it for their own and quickly forgot where they got it.

But as I exercise my imagination on all these matters, my thoughts circle around one person, and that's the fisherman who was observed in Macedonia. Aelian didn't observe him; someone else did. For all we know, the observation passed through several hands, kicking around Eastern Europe for a few years, before reaching Aelian. Maybe it was written down centuries earlier, and he cribbed it from an older source that is now lost. For all we know, it wasn't even accurate or true.

But we still assume it more or less described something that actually happened, and it all does sound plausible. It seems probable that somewhere, one day, barely visible now through the fog of all that hand-me-down information, a specific person stood on a specific Macedonian streambank with a specific fly that he cast or tossed or suspended out over a specific reach of water. That person is pretty hard to feel connected to, but so far, in our woefully incomplete chronicle of the sport's past, he (or she?) is the original unknown fly fisher.

In the two millennia or so of fly fishing that followed, I can think of no one with whom I'd rather spend an afternoon on the river. Give me appropriate dress and tackle, and the ability to speak whatever language I'd need, and I'd be happy to follow Aelian's angler around. I'd love to see him work the riffles and get a look at that fly, the line, the fish, the whole scene. For all the hundreds of fishing books I've read and the dozens of rivers I've fished, I'm sure I'd learn something on a day like that.

CHAPTER NINE

Dogma and the Dry Fly

It is both humbling and a little scary to admit that you've been involved in anything long enough to perceive the long, bumbling haul of history in action. This story takes me back to 1970 or so, at the dawn of the modern fly-fishing revolution. If you've been at this three decades or more, you may remember being taught some version of these simple rules or near commandments: Wet flies are fished downstream. Dry flies are fished upstream. Some strange geniuses will fish wet flies upstream, but you mere mortals shouldn't expect to get much good at that. Nobody fishes dry flies downstream. In fact, it can't be done.

These guidelines were pronounced with an almost moral force: If you foolishly fished a dry fly downstream, not only would you fail to catch fish, but lightning would strike you or you would go blind.

Casting a fly upstream is generally and mistakenly held to be a discovery of the nineteenth century, usually credited to William Stewart in *The Practical Angler* (1857). As Andrew Herd has abundantly demonstrated in his wonderful history of fly fishing, *The Fly* (2001), anglers have been fishing upstream for centuries. Fly fishers have cast upstream whenever it seemed like the right thing to do. By the time Stewart published his book, a lively dialogue was already under way among other writers of his time, and presumably among nonwriting fly fishers as well, about which was best.

The more rational participants in this little feud seemed to feel as we do today: that you cast where you stand the best chance of catching the fish, and it might be up, down, or across. Considering that these people were fishing their flies on or within a few inches of the surface and had been doing so for centuries, it is all the more remarkable what happened to fly fishing in the closing years of the nineteenth century, when the dry fly grew in social stature and technique into something much more clearly defined than it had been before.

The man most often credited—or blamed—for the well-known "dry-fly dogma" was the British writer Frederic Halford. His handsome and confidently pronounced books established the code of dry-fly fishing that prevailed among his associates and would come to rule angling's elevated social circles in early-twentieth-century England. Curious as it seems now, considering the eventual bigotry of his most passionate acolytes when they attacked other types of fly fishing, in Halford we also find some modest indications of open-mindedness. In *Dry-Fly Fishing, Theory and Practice* (1889), Halford revealed some sympathy for fishing downstream:

> Sometimes an extra strong down-stream wind will be blowing with almost hurricane force, rendering it well-nigh impossible, or at best very difficult, to cast up against the wind, even with the under-handed cast or downward cut. Occasionally, too, there are places where, owing to natural obstructions such as trees, bushes, or a jutting promontory just in the range of the line behind the angler, there is no alternative but to drift or throw directly downstream to a fish rising under the fisherman's own bank, or to pass him by altogether. Under such conditions, and such conditions only, it is advisable to drift to a feeding trout or grayling, although in gin-clear water such as the Hampshire chalk streams a very small modicum of success must at the best be anticipated, and no dry-fly fisherman, even the most experienced, need be astonished at finding himself setting down fish after fish, and perhaps not even succeeding in rising a single one during the whole day.

Well, it's a start. But it was a pretty left-handed concession to the approach, wasn't it? In essence, according to Halford, you might like to experiment with downstream drys, and it's okay to do so, but these exceptional circumstances will just prove the rule that the technique doesn't work. So go home and come back when the wind lets up.

America's early dry-fly authorities pretty much bought this. Samuel Camp, in *Fishing with Floating Flies* (1913), personified the absolutism of the upstream dry-fly angler, saying that the dry-fly fisher really "has no option in the matter; regardless of all other factors for upstream fishing, the practical fact remains that the floating fly cannot be fished downstream for when thus cast it is drowned almost at once."

Some prominent American anglers rebelled against this rigid rule. Just as they were doing by developing their own dry-fly patterns even in Halford's day, at least a few Americans would declare their independence from

Despite folklore and expert advice to the contrary, fly fishers have been successfully fishing up-, across-, and downstream with both floating and sunk flies for centuries, as circumstance required. Phil Hanyok drifts a dry fly above a snag on Clark Creek, Pennsylvania.

this element of the dry-fly code. Ray Bergman, in his famed *Trout* (1938), insisted that there were good ways to fish downstream and that "one doesn't hear so much about fishing downstream with a dry fly, but this doesn't alter the fact that the method is important." A. J. McClane, in his wonderfully foresightful primer, *The Practical Fly Fisherman* (1953), described the necessary slack-line cast technique for downstream dry-fly fishing. Joe Brooks's *Trout Fishing* (1972), the first great successor to Bergman's *Trout*, expanded on the concept, even giving us a couple very helpful pages of advice on getting the most out of downstream drifts and the best way to handle the line.

Though it is always a little risky to suggest that the writers of any generation in some meaningful way reflect general public attitudes about anything, I do assume that practical writers like Bergman, McClane, and

Brooks stand for many practical anglers of their times who fished dry flies downstream because it worked. Today we have books such as John Judy's *Slack Line Strategies for Fly Fishing* (1994), large portions of which advise us on making extremely long, effective downstream casts.

But it is still true that when I began fly fishing in 1970s, there was still a widespread conviction, at least in the books I read and the slide presentations I attended, that the dry fly was pretty much an upstream tool. From the beginning, even when completely ignorant of this historical dialogue, I never understood the reported problem with fishing dry flies downstream. Having received almost all of my early fishing instruction from a highly opinionated freestone stream that insisted I learn to catch fish by catching fish, I began violating the upstream code almost immediately. I did this because I had to and because it worked.

It wasn't until I began to read the right books that I discovered how barbaric and unsuccessful my approach was doomed to be. For example, "The dry fly must float naturally, an effect almost impossible to obtain downstream." When as traveled and educated a fly fisher as John McDonald, author of some of the most deservedly acclaimed historical studies in American fly fishing, wrote that uncompromising statement in 1972 in *Quill Gordon*, I was baffled. What was I missing here? How could I have gotten it so wrong and still been so successful? Was it the fault of the trout in my home stream, fish far too dependent on evolutionary imperatives and not nearly respectful enough of the great fishing writers? Or did I just not understand something? These are the moments that give the bookish young fisherman fits.

I stuck with it, though. In the thirty-some years since I started resisting the advice of my betters on downstream dry-fly fishing, my own fishing has changed quietly and completely. Just this past summer it suddenly dawned on me that not only had I gradually become more and more comfortable with downstream drys, but I also now fish them more than upstream drys. All summer, it seemed to me that every time I bothered to notice, I was fishing downstream. Whether from a drift boat or gravel bar, over a deep run or bright riffle, casting downstream just seemed the right thing to do.

It was simple common sense, applied day after day on the stream. I find a rising fish or a likely spot; I read the water to see where the best drift would come from; I go there; I cast. More often than not, I'm casting downstream. I see other fishermen doing this too, people far better at catching fish than I. In what historians would consider a very short time, we've gone from "it's just not done" to "it's just done."

There has to be a lesson in the rapid conversion the sport has undergone. Why did it take us so long to recognize the obvious value of the downstream cast? Halford's dismissal of the technique is bewildering. The obvious advantage of a cast in which the fly comes into the trout's view even before the line does apparently was lost on him. The frequent occasions when line mending is easier on a downstream drift—at least 50 percent of the time, I imagine—must have eluded him too. The greater ease of handling the line as it drifts away from me rather than toward me may just be my own opinion, but it's an opinion I'm very sure of.

Halford's conviction that fishing downstream meant the fish would always see you and thus not rise was even more bewildering. It went against several centuries' experience of countless downstream wet-fly fishermen, people whose flies were often just barely below the surface on their downstream casts. If fish couldn't be caught by fishing downstream, how had all those thousands of wet-fly fishermen done it so well? Skues, looking back on Halford's writings years after his death, summed it up by saying: "Halford did not really understand the wet fly. . . . Of the essential honesty of his opinions there can be no question. His misfortune was that he had not been brought up on, or even had the genuine wet-fly experience, which could have corrected his opinions."

Notice that I'm not criticizing Halford and his cronies just because they liked to make rules. Within the generous limits established by the law, we're all entitled to decide what style of fishing suits us personally, and if upstream dry flies are your preference, more power to you; it's a fine game. But Halford said more. He said the reason not to fish downstream was because it didn't work. There he got my attention and eventually my disregard.

Halford's local circumstances, on his manicured private chalkstreams, may have contributed to his convictions; perhaps my freestone trout, hovering under a broken surface several boulders across the water from me, are more susceptible to a downstream dry. But I've fished enough glassy spring creeks to doubt that it was as simple as Halford thought it was, even on his home water.

The rise of the downstream dry fly shouldn't be that big a surprise. Anglers of each generation tend to shed some of their predecessors' dogma, to stake their own claim to the sport, to take up the challenge in a fresh way, or just to prove that they're smarter than their parents.

On the other hand, each generation also has its dropouts, anglers who settle in with a certain set of rules and stick to them. Even though I fish dry flies downstream and do plenty of other things on the water that were unfashionable fifty years ago, I'm also gradually being left behind. My fly rods, though most are made of graphite, are many years and numerous new models behind the current latest thing, and I don't care. These rods may be old enough to vote, but they have the capacity for casts far beyond my skills. If my casting were ever to catch up—and it won't—I'd think about buying new ones.

More important, I ignore significant portions of today's fly-fishing practice, things that for all their allure and energy just don't work for me. I catch fewer fish than I would if I embraced all these things, but I catch my fish in a way that suits me.

Strike detectors, now universal on fashionable trout streams, never seemed quite okay to me. They were too much like the bobbers I used long ago for catching bluegills with cane poles; they crossed some threshold that put me off, and not just an aesthetic one. True, I didn't like that blobby little interruption of the fly line's continuous and very meaningful taper. But I didn't really like the extra edge it seemed to give me either, even though strike detectors could mean the difference between catching fish and having blank days. These things, these little subjective decisions, are what make the whole business matter to us, each in our own way.

The same goes for beadhead patterns, all those otherwise pretty flies with a big, shiny brass ball ruining their proportions. I used to use them sometimes. I have a lot of them in my wet-fly box, and once in a while I still give one a try, but most of mine look like new. I just don't like them. And I'm pleased to notice the company I keep in that opinion. In *Good Flies* (2000), John Gierach expresses the same view:

> I know they're popular, I know they catch fish, and I've even used them a few times, usually to keep from insulting a guide or a friendly fisherman who insisted that a bead-head something-or-other was the only fly that would work. I just think they're ugly, so I can't bring myself to tie them, but it's nothing personal.

Aesthetics have been as important in fly fishing as have pragmatic mechanics. The beadhead fly, now universally popular and very effective on trout streams, was a dramatic departure from traditional ideals of proportion and imitation in fly tying. The line between a fly and a lure has been neither stationary nor easily determined. ILLUSTRATION BY MARSHA KARLE.

Well, it's nothing personal against the other fishermen. But, it's everything personal for those of us who decide that this particular type of fly just doesn't fit our needs as fly fishers.

Those of us who decide not to add some new thing to our fly fishing are part of that tension between classicism and innovation that John McDonald described, which seems to be an interesting and energizing part of the sport. Even Halford went from representing the innovators to symbolizing the classicists in only a couple decades. Sometimes the tradition has a pretty fast turnover.

I don't deny that we could catch more fish if we embraced every trick that came down the pike. It's just that some of those things cross some faint but hard line for many of us. Halford's disdain for downstream dry flies isn't really that different from mine for beadheads, except that he thought downstream drys wouldn't work. By contrast, I don't even care whether beadheads work. I just think they look stupid and miss some subtle ideal in the whole point of using flies in the first place. Who's to say which is the more problematic bias?

Maybe we each get our turn at being an old coot. We go from discovering fly fishing, when everything about it is new to us and we fall in love with its funny little ways, to getting comfortable with the sport as we found it. Then it begins to change out from under us, and each time some new change sweeps in off the highways of commerce and innovation, we have to decide whether to go along for the ride or hop off and stick with what we know.

CHAPTER TEN

The Visible Hook

Fly tiers, even those who are new to the craft, probably share at least one common experience. For some of us, it may happen the first day we sit down at the vise. For others, the combination of absorption and exasperation of fly tying may keep us from thinking too hard about it for a long time. But eventually all of us must look at a pattern we have just finished tying—even one that seems especially promising—and wonder something like this: "Well, it looks good, but what trout in its right mind would be fooled by an insect imitation with that big shiny hook hanging out its butt?"

It's a good question. It may even be a big question. After all, if trout are as sophisticated and canny as our hatch-matching technicians make them out to be, that hook should put every single one of them off their feed. How is it that a spring creek trout you spend half an hour working on, a fish that rejects every fly pattern you try and gives every appearance of great skill at visual discrimination of color, shape, and size, demands that you throw it just the right imitation of just the right insect but is willing to tolerate that big, unnatural metal hook?

I must admit, for me this has always seemed a much more mystifying puzzle than a trout's willingness to take a fly attached to a leader, even the big, thick leaders that I use. When I started fishing, I used to worry a lot about leaders, just as I had been taught in many of the best fishing books. But one day in Oregon about thirty years ago, as I was agonizing over some monofilament issues, my steelhead-fishing friend Dale Greenley shook his head impatiently and said, "The fish doesn't know what that leader is."

I hadn't even thought about that. Dale's assertion tidily summed up a complex circumstance of animal consciousness. We have no reason to assume that a fish understands that a line attached to a fly has a fisherman on the other end. We have no reason to assume that a fish even understands the idea of attachment, much less the notion that an attached line is something that can be pulled on. What stake can the trout have in the leader, as long as it's not affecting the behavior of the fly?

On the other hand, the trout is deciding whether to eat the fly. That's about as personal a stake as the trout can have in anything. So why does the fish still eat an artificial fly with a hook hanging out of it, even though it is so visibly unlike the natural flies around it? Why doesn't the trout mind the hook?

Anglers in Denial

The past few centuries of fishing writers were pretty quiet on this discomforting reality. Some of them wondered about it. In 1857, William Stewart pointed out in *The Practical Angler* that "a fly with the exposed part of the hook taken off, will raise more trout than a fly with the same left on." But being practical types, most fishermen apparently just set the whole issue aside. If somebody asked someone else about it, he probably said, "How am *I* supposed to know what the trout thinks, and why should I care as long as it takes the fly?" The hook, after all, was necessary. Why spend a lot of time agonizing over it?

And that's a fair question. Flies work. Even with dry flies, which feature greatly complicated underwater visual challenges for the trout because of the messy physics of light interacting with a dimpled, dented, and otherwise distorted surface, it's a sure thing that the fish often gets a very good look at the hook. For the most pragmatic of us, as well as for the intellectually stunted, that's good enough. It's a sure thing that the bend, point, and eye of the hook, though exposed to the full view of the fish in most patterns, don't stop the fish from taking the fly.

Or it might be more accurate to say that they don't stop *some* fish from taking the fly. We simply don't know what role these very visible elements of the hook play in preventing the takes of all the fish we *don't* catch. And in our darker moments, we know that our flies either miss or fail to attract the interest of many fish for every one we actually hook. So even if the entertainment of open-ended theoretical inquiry doesn't draw you into this subject, you might want to stick with this investigation for practical reasons.

Consider this: Maybe all along it's been the hook, rather than the wrong shade of tail fibers or a poorly shaped thorax or an improperly seated wing

Though it is obvious that a fly line can spook a fish, it is far less clear that the fish in any way associates the line it sees with the fisherman holding on to the other end of it. David Ledlie almost dapping on Cress Spring Creek, Montana.

127

Almost every successful cast is to some extent a testament to a fly pattern that, for whatever mysterious reason, persuaded a trout to ignore a hook. Bob DeMott setting the hook in a large trout on Benhart Creek, Montana.

or an incorrectly colored body, that's been making so many of our imitations unsuccessful all these years. Maybe hooks do matter. Maybe they matter a lot.

For some of the twentieth century's best angling writers, the issue of hook visibility was interesting, even intriguing, but not especially resolvable. G. E. M. Skues, who seems to have thought harder and better than most other fly-fishing writers about most of the important questions, kept an open mind to the extent of nearly admitting that he really didn't have a clue what the trout made of the hook. Like most of us, he was result-oriented. As he said in *The Way of a Trout with a Fly* (1921) of the visible hook:

> It does not deter trout from frequently seeking to make a meal of the artificial fly. The trout, therefore, must either fail to see the hook, or seeing it, must ignore it. If he sees it and realizes that it is an unnatural appendage to the artificial fly, he could hardly ignore it. He must therefore either take it for a natural appendage, or for some casual, but quite irrelevant, attachment, or be so obsessed by his intentness on his food as to see only what he wants.

Recognizing that all sorts of flotsam could become attached to a living insect, or even possibly some kind of living thing, such as a tiny leech, Skues still leaned toward the theory that the trout was so enslaved to the feeding urge that "he sees only what he wants to see." This led Skues to the happy if startling conclusion that "the wily trout of the poets and journalists is—may Providence be devoutly thanked for it—really rather a stupid person."

Others have echoed Skues's general mood. It could be that the trout thinks the hook is some sort of appendage—maybe the remains of a nymphal shuck, an unusually long abdomen curled under the body, the trailing effects of some injury, or just some stream junk that happened by. Most of us don't imagine that the trout is able to think out precisely such alternatives, but we can agree that the trout sees little unnatural or alarming in the hook's being there.

Skues and other writers that followed him were stumbling toward a greater truth. J. W. Dunne, in *Sunshine and the Dry Fly* (1924), advanced Skues's position by emphasizing that a trout that sees "only what he wants to see" was in fact being something other than willfully stupid. Drawing on his understanding of human psychology, Dunne said, "I think we can all agree to this: If we are looking around for some particular thing, we shall notice points of resemblance to that thing before we notice points of difference." He then asserted:

> The more elementary the mind, the more potent in effect are such characteristics. For the trout, then, resemblances count for even more than they do with us. And a trout examining objects passing overhead for the one thing he is looking for—that colour effect which spells "fly"—will not only notice, as we do, the points of resemblance first and the differences afterwards, but will be far more impressed than we should be by such points of resemblance as he sees. And his limited mind will concentrate on these to the detriment of his attention towards such extraneous trappings as hooks, or gut, or superfluous legs.

Behavioral Patterns

Modern students of animal behavior and consciousness wouldn't necessarily buy Skues's rather pointed value judgment on the trout's "stupid" failure to grasp the significance of the hook. It wasn't stupidity that enabled the trout family to survive for so many millions of years. The trout behaves the way it does because its evolution has been eminently successful. It's just that all those eons of survival in the wild couldn't be expected to prepare it, or any other species, for the evolutionary loose cannon that is technological humanity. That's hardly the trout's fault.

Animal behaviorists, beginning especially at midcentury with the work of the brilliant Nobel laureate Niko Tinbergen, developed formal language to describe what goes on when an animal is looking for food. Specifically, a fish or any other animal that establishes a preference for a certain food necessarily develops a search image for it, a mental tool enabling the creature to efficiently pick the preferred item from its visual field. Consider, by comparison, our ever-present if latent search image for a $20 bill that allows us to instantly and involuntarily identify and concentrate on one lying anywhere within our visual range.

Though not all of it agrees with the search image concept, there is now a sizable scientific literature on the complex process by which predators go about the even more complicated business of choosing among several or many available prey species. It points out the evident advantages to the predator of tending to concentrate on one of the available species to the near exclusion of the others—what we think of as a trout's "selectivity."

The trout's attention to a certain prey image allows it to distinguish the fly from everything else around it—perhaps, Dunne's theory might suggest, even from things that are attached to it. In this case, it would seem, the trout's skill at focusing on a certain type of prey can backfire if the focus keeps it from paying attention to other things, like the hook.

Based on gradual improvements in our thinking and our scientific vocabulary, we have been revisiting trout feeding habits ever since Skues and Dunne thought about them. In *The Way of the Trout* (1991), Monty Montgomery lived up to the obligation incurred by so nearly copying the title of Skues's earlier masterpiece with a long discussion of how trout decide what to eat and what to reject and why it seemed to him that certain great fly patterns honored the trout's natural imperatives. As far as the problem of the visible hook, Montgomery pointed out:

> The first assumption you can make about trout is that they ignore things. Even a very small hook has a gap considerably larger than the eye of a trophy trout: try to imagine tricking a sentient being into eating a chocolate-covered cherry that has a shiny metal hook as wide as the human eyeball sticking out of it. You would be very surprised if you succeeded.

What may be most important in this statement is the recognition of the trout's capacity for ignoring what it has no evolutionary reason to notice. This brings us to the shape of the hook itself. All of those clever ways we anglers have contrived to obscure the trout's view of the hook—from the well-threaded night crawler on a big Eagle Claw to a hundred variations on reverse-tied, short-shanked, long-bearded, overhackled, small-gaped, trailing-winged, keel-hooked patterns—often seem to suggest that we imagine the trout will recognize the threat the hook poses and will know that because of its shape, it has a lethal purpose and must be avoided. But we have no reason to give the trout credit for such an advanced understanding of human technology.

What the fishing writers and animal behaviorists were getting at is this: The trick to understanding why the trout takes a hook is in *not* thinking like a human who sees the hook in the chocolate-covered cherry. In *My Friend the Trout* (1961), Eugene Connett III said, "We must remember that trout don't know that there is such a thing as a hook, and they are therefore not looking for one when they see what they take to be a natural insect." And Connett rightly pointed out that even a fish that has been caught and released a few times, though it may now associate the hook with a certain risk and tend to avoid it, still may have no understanding whatsoever of the way in which hooks work. The smartened-up trout may be only "more suspicious and particular about the appearance of flies than his less experienced brother; which is usually why we find him more difficult to catch."

It's all so hard to pin down. Perhaps the trout's caution has nothing to do with the hook. Perhaps it's something else in the appearance of the artificial. Perhaps it's really the line that triggers the fish's caution after it has been caught once or more. Does a struggling trout ever get a good enough look at the line to see that it goes directly to a rod and fisherman? If it saw that, would it know what it means? Or perhaps it's not even the same thing in each case.

The experiments of a number of anglers, including me, with catching the occasional trout on a bare hook also seem to buttress the idea that the hook is not an inherently scary shape in a trout's mind. So far, these are my foremost conclusions in this quixotic venture of fishing with a plain or even a colored hook: It's a long time between strikes; once in a great while, for whatever reason, an unadorned hook meets a trout's definition of "worth a try"; and even less often, in fact much less often, trout actually seem to like a flyless hook.

It could also be argued that the reason we catch so few fish on bare hooks is that a hook with no furs or feathers obscuring it is even scarier than one hidden in an artificial fly. But I doubt that. I think that a bare hook, even one painted an attractive color, just doesn't look enough like anything edible to be attractive to a lot of fish.

Goofy but intriguing stunts like fishing with bare hooks aside, our growing understanding of trout and the science of animal behavior has led to what seems to me a kind of modern synthesis on the hook question.

It is best summed up by Andrew Herd, who looks at the long haul of theorizing on this question and, rather like Dunne, turns it on its head, concluding that it's not the wrongness of the visible hook that matters most—it's the rightness of everything else about the artificial fly. As Herd puts it, "If enough triggers are incorporated in a pattern, most fish will ignore evidence to the contrary such as hook bends." If you get enough things right about the fly pattern, the hook becomes irrelevant. Get the fly pattern and presentation close enough to satisfy the trout's expectations and it simply overrides any doubts it may have about the hook, line, or leader. That may seem intuitive, but any experienced spring-creek fisherman will tell you that it's not simple.

Horridly Conspicuous Necessities

Hooks have occupied the attention of anglers as along they have understood what an angle was and how to put it to use in water. There are tens of thousands of kinds of hooks, made from materials and in shapes beyond counting. Over the years, we have tried a lot of ways to make the hook less visible. Besides all the ways we've tried to hide the hook behind wings and hackles and whatnot, we've played endlessly with alternative shapes, dabbled in colored hooks, and even approached the dream of clear ones. But practically all of us still use pretty much the same kinds of hooks as our grandfathers did, at least as far as general characteristics such as color, thickness, and style.

Some of the experiments we've tried have been intriguing, though. E. W. Harding, author of the great foundation book on the trout's perception, *The Flyfisher & the Trout's Point of View* (1931), was one of many anglers since the late 1800s to examine flies through a glass-sided tank especially constructed for the purpose. Admitting that "most anglers regard the hook as a horridly conspicuous necessity and wonder how the trout can tolerate it," Harding conducted a few general experiments, also admitting that a lot more work would have to be done before his findings were proven conclusive. He wondered about matching the hook to the prevailing light conditions on the river instead of to the artificial fly pattern tied on it. After experimenting with bronzed and nickel-plated hooks, he concluded that under certain subdued light conditions, the mirrorlike reflectivity of the nickel-plated hook, rather than causing it to shine like a chrome hubcap, actually made it hard to see:

> With the light behind them and sunk a little below the surface, both
> sorts of hook are inconspicuous. The threadlike core of the bronzed
> hook takes up an olive tone slightly darker than the rest of the water,

while the nickel-plated hook seems to reflect its surroundings completely. When the sun is straight ahead and low down, it is very difficult to see the nickel-plated hook at all. This is exactly in accordance with the theory of the subject. In diffused light it should be nearly a perfect mirror and reflect its surroundings almost completely. It does, and so is practically invisible. When facing a direct light, it should reflect it and so flash. It does, and therefore it shows up.

It may be an advantage, then, to use nickel-plated hooks when the sun is well in front of the fish, especially in thin shallow water where there is not enough colour from reflected light to tone the bronzed hook into its environment. More generally, wherever the part of the hook which the trout may see is in diffused light and not exposed to the direct rays, it is probably an advantage to use nickel-plated hooks. But when the sun is behind the trout, the part of the hook visible to him is exposed to direct rays of light, then the bronzed hook is preferable. This is a small detail only, one of many, but it may just make the difference between a fish or two or none at all.

The disadvantage of this system is that it assumes that the angler will not change direction relative to the fish. If you were winding your way along a trout stream, fishing this way and that, from one bank and then the other, you'd constantly be changing flies so that your hook matched the appropriate angle of the sunlight. Maybe Harding had the patience for that, but I wouldn't.

Though I realize it wasn't the same thing and involved anadromous fish whose feeding impulse is something of a bafflement to us anyway, discussions of exposed hooks always bring to mind Jock Scott's *Greased Line Fishing for Salmon* (1933), with its account of the low-water "patterns" known as Blueshanks and Redshanks, which were just bare hooks with the shank painted one color for most of its length. I suppose his book helped inspire my own current distraction with "fly fishing" with bare hooks.

Considering the huge amount of theorizing that has long gone into trying to determine the correct color for fly lines and leaders, it seems odd that we fly fishers have given the appearance, color, and reflectivity of the hook so little thought. It seems even more odd that we've sometimes developed hook color standards that openly defy any theory of camouflage, such as the requisite black of traditional Atlantic salmon flies. Maybe this is because, like all those centuries of anglers before us, we have just accepted the hook as a given—as a necessary part of the deal, "horridly conspicuous" though it may be. Or maybe it's just part of the aesthetics of a sport that has made an obsession of fishing in a certain way simply because that way was most satisfying, rather than because it would result

*Though concealing the hook may not always
have been their primary goal, fly tiers have
found many ways to accomplish
that camouflage. The Bivisible, as
popularized and perhaps even originated
by Edward Hewitt, is hackled the entire length
of the hook shank, which surely obscures the
hook's bend to some extent.*

*The Renegade, the most popular American
fore-and-aft-style dry fly, likewise obscures
the hook in hackles.*

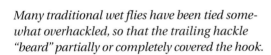

*Many traditional wet flies have been tied some-
what overhackled, so that the trailing hackle
"beard" partially or completely covered the hook.*

*The Dabbler, developed and popularized by the
Irish fly tier Donald McClearn in the 1990s, com-
bines generously long hackles, lightly palmered
the length of the body, with even longer mallard
flank feathers tied in small clumps on the top
and sides to further cloak the body and
hook. Many British and Irish loch
flies are tied with what seem to
the American eye to be excessively
long wings, hackles, or legs. If the hook
is not actually hidden, it may be visually
lost in the profusion of other fibers.*

134

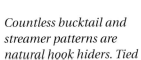

Countless bucktail and streamer patterns are natural hook hiders. Tied with a beard as long as the wing, the fly has a smooth profile from which the hook may or may not protrude. See Carrie Stevens's Gray Ghost on page 158 for another excellent streamer style that hid most of the hook bend.

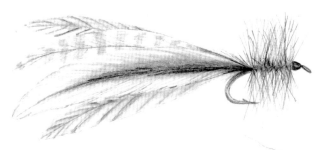

Homer Rhode Jr.'s saltwater streamer, with its densely palmered hook shank and long, trailing wing, probably provides enough distractions from the hook even if it isn't always fully concealed.

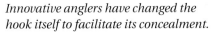

Innovative anglers have changed the hook itself to facilitate its concealment. The keel hook, the most popular of several historical attempts to develop an upside-down fly, has been marketed primarily for its weedless capabilities, but its obvious potential for hiding the hook point is another advantage of the style.

Fly tiers have been experimenting with various kinds of extended bodies on dry flies for many years, but using that approach intentionally to conceal the hook point is a more recent development. The Fly Body hook, introduced in the 1970s, permitted tiers to honor the conventional proportions of the dry fly while placing the hook point under the hackles. ILLUSTRATIONS BY MARSHA KARLE.

in the most pounds of food to eat. This kind of fatalistic reasoning has often been good enough for me when I have to decide how I shall fly-fish.

Still, it would be interesting if a few die-hard empiricists out there were to reconsider the hook in light of the wealth of knowledge we now have of natural and military camouflage and even stealth technology. Could hooks be given an uneven enough surface texture to break up light reflectivity in some helpful way? Could we apply all we now know about fish vision to the color of hooks? Would it help my Light Cahill's effectiveness if the pale body color continued partway around the bend of the hook? Would it help to countershade the hook through its bend, making it lighter underneath and darker above?

I don't doubt that some hook specialists, far better informed than I about the technological possibilities, have already been asking these and many other questions. But I do wonder why we haven't heard more from them. Not that I would necessarily jump on their bandwagon. I fall into that category of moderately tradition-minded anglers who tend to like some of the limitations we inherited from earlier generations.

But at the same time, I'm enormously curious about how trout work. Even if their minds are limited and they are in fact rather stupid, they're still vastly interesting animals to deal with—especially on the terms that fly fishing demands of us. By the standards of all previous generations, modern hooks are superb. Maybe our hooks are as good as they'll ever get. They're certainly good enough to suit me. But good enough has rarely sufficed in fly fishing, so I'm a little surprised we seem to have settled for it in the matter of hook theory.

CHAPTER ELEVEN

Hackles

Thanks to my fishing diary, I know exactly when this happened. On the evening of July 27, 1976, having just read Sylvester Nemes's book *The Soft-Hackled Fly* (1975) and tied up a batch of his favorites, I waded into my neighborhood trout stream with the usual low expectations—everybody catches lots of trout in books, right?

Later that evening, after having my most successful fishing in five years on that stream, I waded out a convert. I would always have some of these flies, and this gent Nemes would always have at least one customer for his next book. And it's true. I always have some soft-hackles, more all the time. And I continue to buy his books, including all four that Nemes has published on soft-hackled flies.

A couple winters ago, having been away from tying for far too long, I eased my way back in by tying up a few hundred soft-hackles. I'm not your slide-show grade of fly tier, and I like tying soft-hackles because they are quick enough that my output satisfies me. Better still, it's almost impossible to tie them so hideously that they won't catch fish. So my enthusiasm for these wonderful patterns was refreshed, and I cast them over many droughty western waters the following summer, where, like all really terrific and especially beloved fly patterns, they worked about as well as anything else.

But during the quarter century between these two experiences, I had fished a lot and read even more. This meant that as I tied away all those snowy evenings, I was no longer content with the imparted wisdom, undeniably wise though it was, about how these flies should look. I experienced a kind of aesthetic epiphany, and I began to question authority as well as taste.

I admit, this discontent had its practical side. Some of my frustration was the fault of grouse, birds so full of their own impertinent needs that they refuse to grow feathers properly sized for the smaller hooks. Like many generations of anglers before me, I struggled with the fly tier's known tricks for downsizing hackles, but I was often tempted by the dark side of disproportion. What if, sacrilege though it be, I just tied the larger hackles on the smaller hooks and, as a song once put it, let it all hang out? Who would know? Would the fish care? And come to think of it, who decided how far these hackles should hang out in the first place?

And another thing. The experts seemed to have this nearly anorexic obsession about extreme lightness of body and sparseness of hackle. There was something perverse about this: If I did finally find a grouse considerate enough to grow tiny hackles, I was supposed to use only one turn of the precious hackle on each fly. There's no luxury in that, and again I wondered: Who said so? Where did these unyielding prescriptions come from?

Soft-Hackle Proportions

Sylvester Nemes's books, as helpful as they have been in introducing a couple generations of fly fishers to soft-hackles, have relatively little to say, either comprehensively or specifically, about the big questions of proportion. You can look at his splendid color photographs of the flies he ties and see how he suggests you make them look, but he gives little background on why hackle lengths are prescribed as they are. His books, like most that are fly related, tend to be pattern dictionaries rather than studies of pattern theory.

But in not talking about proportion in detail, Nemes is just honoring the general tradition of writing on these flies. Though some of the important writers on soft-hackled flies may have provided prescriptions on basic proportions, they said little about why those proportions were the right ones. Some writers insisted, or at least implied, that the imitation should look like the natural it is supposed to match. They might have given a generalized prescription for this or that element of the fly, such as the common conviction among many writers that the bodies must be very sparsely tied or William Stewart's suggestion that his spider's hackles be about the length of the hook. But unlike the rigid definitions that characterize most other fly styles, the soft-hackles hang pretty loose in the theory department.

It is hackle length that got me into this inquiry and hackle length that interests me the most. If you want to tie a Catskill-style dry fly, every fly-tying book tells you precisely how long the hackles should be. If you want

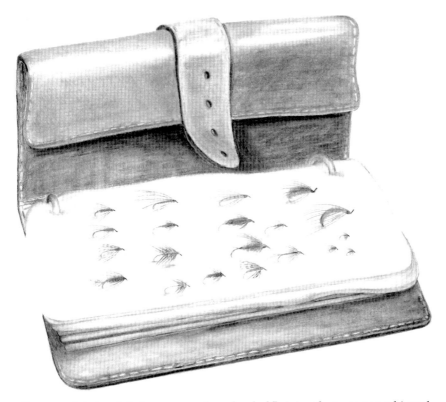

Because of their origin in a vernacular school of fly tying that was not subjected to broad standardization, soft-hackled flies as a type are happily free from strict rules regarding proportion and other characteristics. Few other fly styles invite so much experimentation and variability. ILLUSTRATION BY MARSHA KARLE.

to tie a traditional quill-wing wet fly, you may find a little more variation in hackle length among the patterns, but there is still a clear sense of a proportional "rightness" to be honored. Darrel Martin, in his entertaining book *The Fly Fisher's Illustrated Dictionary* (2000), provides a long, helpful, and well-illustrated discussion of fly proportions and summarizes established conventions on wet flies: The hackles on a quill-wing wet fly "may extend to the hook point, may equal hook gap, or may equal one-half the hook shank." These are all choices within a reasonable stylistic realm. I do not sense that much consistency in the soft-hackle literature.

On average, one gets the impression that soft-hackles are to be tied with hackles somewhat longer than those on traditional winged wet flies, apparently because the legs of the insects being imitated were actually as long as those on the imitation. But beyond that, and considering all the confusion over entomology and its terminology before 1920 or so and the consequent uncertainties about precisely what insects wet flies were supposed to be imitating, it's often hard to know what to make of even the rare general guidelines we were given.

Flies from the North Country

Though it seems reasonably certain now that many European fly fishers, at least since Aelian's time, used similar styles of flies, the first stop on any historical tour of soft-hackle authority and authenticity is a pair of scarce British angling classics, Thomas Evan Pritt's *Yorkshire Trout Flies* (1885) and Harfield Edmonds and Norman Lee's *Brook and River Trouting* (1916). These two short but satisfying books laid out a nice, solid orthodoxy.

But if you stare at their color plates of fly patterns long enough, you notice that there's still some unexplained variation in hackle length and density, and in body size for that matter. If you need formulas, you're in trouble.

It gets worse, because the specialists who have studied the North Country fly-tying tradition would have you know that Pritt, Edmonds, and Lee aren't the real authorities anyway. For hard-core authenticity and originality, you'd better read John Turton's *Angler's Manual* (1836), John Jackson's *Practical Fly-Fisher* (1854), maybe David Webster's *Angler and the Loop Rod* (1885), and half a dozen other books that even our leading fly-fishing writers haven't said much about. Of course, it's assumed that you already have William Stewart's irreplaceable *Practical Angler* (1857), right?

There's a level of original authenticity even beyond these writers. The most serious students of this field of arcana, Leslie Magee, in *Fly Fishing: The North Country Tradition* (1994), and Roger Fogg, in *A Handbook of North Country Trout Flies* (1988), trace the soft-hackle lineage back not just to ever more obscure books, but also to a surprising wealth of unpublished nineteenth-century manuscripts, some containing actual flies or at least drawings of them.

At all these levels of expertise, I have found myself figuratively looking over the shoulder of the author, trying to make sense of the actual flies I could see tucked away in the corner of this or that illustration. Their hackles are all over the map, so to speak, and quite a few flies have bodies that are nothing short of tubby, so I returned from this literary trip with a whole new appreciation of the soft-hackled fly as a dynamic and lively idea.

The most obvious answer to my befuddlement is that each fly pattern was originated in response to a certain insect, group of insects, or theory of insects. Naturally, some are fatter than others; some have longer legs than others. Some have other personality quirks. Of course the fly patterns look different—the real insects do too.

The North Country tradition, which gave us our most popular soft-hackled fly patterns, includes much more than the famous wingless ones we now know best. William Stewart's Practical Angler *(1857), often cited as among the most important works on fishing such flies on the rugged freestone streams where the tradition developed, pictured three dramatically different styles.*

On the left is Stewart's "spider." Contrary to the prevailing tendency among more recent soft-hackle authorities, it was tied semipalmer, with about half the hook shank covered by the soft hackle but no body, wing, or tail. The term "spider" was later used to describe the lightly hackled soft-hackled flies we now associate with the type and was also applied to a certain class of dry flies.

In the middle is a fly dressed with only a wing and short, sparse, dubbed body. It has no hackle at all; the dubbing was picked out with a needle to create a feathery appearance behind the head.

On the right is an equally sparse fly with a short, thin, dubbed body and one or two turns of soft hackle at the head; the hackles are perhaps half the length of the hook. Many later North Country writers abandoned wings almost entirely, but Stewart was devoted to them, in part because he believed that a winged fly held together longer under hard use than a simple hackled fly.

This figuring out of proportion might be a lot simpler if all we were trying to do was get the hackle length right to match the proportionate leg lengths on corresponding caddis pupae, this being the group of insects most often said to be the originals or naturals of soft-hackled flies. But we use soft-hackles in all sorts of other situations, when we suspect that the trout are probably feeding on mayflies, stoneflies, scuds, and so on. The good Mr. Nemes, obviously a creative and resourceful angler, has even tied soft-hackles purposely to represent other insect types and to fish both wet and more or less dry.

Now and then, prescriptions for style and proportion did emerge, even in this free-for-all tradition. Besides differences in hackle length, fly-tying traditions developed on individual rivers dictated dramatically different body lengths. W. H. Lawrie's *Scottish Trout Flies* (1966), for example, pointed out that anglers on three different Scottish river basins independently developed body styles that were quite distinct from one another: On the Tweed, bodies were the full length of the hook shank; on the Clyde, they were half-shank length; and on the Tummel, they were barely as long as the thorax portion of a modern nymph pattern. It seems pretty unlikely that such dramatic differences in tying style had a lot to do with the corresponding proportions of the insects on those streams, but maybe somehow they did.

Andrew Herd was the first to warn me about the happy messiness of the North Country fly-tying tradition: "What we are looking at here is a truly vernacular school, which didn't suffer the indignity of literary attention until it was so well established that it had been taken for granted." In other words, the soft-hackled fly, lacking the kind of standardization that widespread literary and commercial popularity would lead to, experienced parallel evolution on many British rivers, and even its most successful formalizers, well-respected types like Pritt, couldn't overcome that local independence.

Thank heaven for that. It's kind of liberating to read books by these early North Country anglers now. This literature is Quirk Central. One writer might insist that for fast water, you really need to tie a good, stiff rooster hackle right behind the soft grouse (or snipe, or starling, or whatever) hackle to help prop it out away from the body of the fly. Another might just as firmly believe that even in fast water, the softest hackles will reliably unplaster themselves from the hook shank and work their magic.

The Cutcliffe Variation

Perhaps the most remarkable example of the individuality of approach among North Country fly theorists is provided by H. C. Cutcliffe, who wrote *The Art of Trout Fishing on Rapid Streams* (1863). Though later writers typically group Cutcliffe with the soft-hackled fly authorities and North Country writers, they do so because there seems no place else to put him. The North Devon streams he fished meet almost no one's definition of the North Country, and more important, his hackles weren't soft.

Cutcliffe had little use for wings, which is one way his flies do fit the modern soft-hackle stereotype. He complained that typical wet-fly wings stick to the body of the fly once wet, causing the fly to look "more like a little roll of the dung of a rat than a fly." Nice imagery.

But in other ways, he departed from the loose orthodoxy of the North Country tradition completely. Instead of the webby, nimble feathers of partridge and other typical soft-hackle feathers, he was almost exclusively devoted to rooster hackles:

> All hackles should be plucked from a cock's neck; hens' hackles are worse than useless in rapid streams; they have no stiffness, cannot resist the force of the water washing on them, and consequently lie flat

along the hook, lose all the little colour they have when dry, and make your fly hook look more like a little oval black mass of dirt, rather than a living insect.

Cutcliffe was passionately convinced that only the stiffest hackles could withstand the swift currents of freestone streams. His advice sounds exactly like later dry-fly experts coaching readers to find only the brightest, stiffest hackles available. His warm discussions of the luster, colors, and "richness of tinge" of Old English gamecocks match any later appreciations of those feathers I've read and exceed most.

He was equally passionate about mixing a great variety of natural furs to match those feathers. His goal was to create a fly whose hackle and body were studies in a complex blend of tints that remind me of John Atherton's impressionistic fly patterns of almost a century later. Listen to his excitement over making these involved combinations of tints work together and you realize that some of our long-dead predecessors were no less sophisticated or subtle fly theorists than we are today:

> By choosing a red bantam we shall ensure a richness of tinge in our hackle, and procure more rusty blues and reds than plain and sober coloured feathers. These rusty feathers are by far the most rare, and by far the best when obtained; they combine several colours, and shot as it were over the surface of a rich glossy grounding in blue and red, and on scrutinizing their surface carefully we perceive the exact similarities in tints of shading to the natural colour of various furs, as the ends of hare's flax, water rat, and mouse and fox fur, pulled out and mixed well together.

One last note on Cutcliffe's special take on these versatile wet flies. Once his hard-hackled wet flies were tied, he would bunch the hackles above and below the hook and pull each bunch between his thumb and a pocketknife blade to train them into gentle arcs, one upward and one downward. He said that the upper bunch then represented the wings and the lower bunch the legs. He admitted that he did not really know whether this had any "practical advantage" in fooling the fish, but he was sure that it gave the bunched fibers a better chance of standing up against the current than if they were simply arrayed all around the hook the way typically wound hackles are.

Despite what Roger Fogg calls Cutcliffe's "Victorian prolixity," his book is full of stimulating thinking and intriguing ideas. But though I'm known for being pretty good at worrying about trivial things, I join the long parade of writers who have never been able to buy into his fear that typical soft-hackles will spend all their underwater time plastered against the fly's body. When I swim a soft-hackle around in the water in front of me on a short leader, the hackles seem to move around and stick out just fine. If I pull the fly very quickly through the water or hold it in place against a stiff current, the hackles may indeed glom onto the body of the fly in imitation of a rat turd. And if I take it out of the water they'll do the same thing. But if I'm drifting the fly along in any reasonable way, even if I'm pulling it slowly through the water, I think I can have a fair amount of faith that the hackles will do their job just fine. Maybe Cutcliffe's "rapid streams" were a lot more rapid than mine.

The General Idea

When you look past the few really well-known and fairly standardized soft-hackle patterns that have achieved popularity in the United States—Partridge and Orange, Snipe and Purple, and so on—there is still surprising flexibility. A good example is Fogg's description in *A Handbook of North Country Trout Flies* of a modern pattern called the Crimson Woodcock, whose body is "crimson tying silk, floss silk or wool. A thorax of peacock herl or red fox produces an attractive fly."

Huh? The body should be smooth silk or fuzzy wool? You can consider an optional thorax that can be made of either peacock or red fox? Nice creative latitude there. Imagine someone exercising that sort of looseness in describing a modern "classic" Catskill dry fly: "Body: stripped peacock herl, unless you would prefer moose mane or vulture biot. Oh, and a little chartreuse floss ribbing is a cheery touch."

One of the most intriguing alternative opinions on just how those long, supple hackles work was provided by E. W. Harding in *The Flyfisher & the Trout's Point of View* (1931), who theorized that in fast water, the hackles didn't really imitate legs so much as suggest a continuous lifelike shape:

> The longish, sparse hackles drawn fairly closely to the body, though not clinging to it, and quivering in the stream would produce the effect of misty fringes. I am not convinced that the usual explanation that the quivering hackles give the effect of a live insect struggling in the stream is altogether right or necessary. The speed of movement in the water which causes light and colour to flicker over the surfaces seen by the trout would so I think, give all the impressions of life that the trout sees in the natural insect.

This idea of Harding's is interesting. Many immature forms of aquatic insects have sides that are at least partly lined with a fine fringe of gills; perhaps those are what the "misty fringes" of the quivering hackles actually suggest. It's another pleasant theory for rumination and experimentation.

144

Because they are routinely fished to drift either in or just beneath the surface, lightly dressed soft-hackles are easily fished upstream exactly as if they were dry flies. Here I am fishing a soft-hackle on the Gibbon River, Yellowstone National Park. PHOTO BY MARSHA KARLE.

My response to the enduring flexibility—and amazing array of local convictions and opinions—of this "school" of fly tying is to embrace its spirit and let the confusing details go. The passionate insistence among so many North Country fly experts on a lightly dressed, lean body is worth respecting, even though it requires me to overcome many years of conditioning that a meaty-looking fly must be a better fly. I've seen those shank-thin, wispy little things work too often to doubt them.

As for the hackle-length bewilderment that got me started on all this, Andrew Herd spoke with authority and took the pressure off when he told me, "I think the only mistake you can make is to have the hackles too long; over 1.5 times the hook length looks weird to me, and under 0.5 seems too short, but what the hell."

Well, okay, allowing me a hackle length variation of 300 percent is fairly painless. At least I'm willing to live with it until the genetic engineers at the hackle companies realize how many of us out here are waiting for them to produce a mutant partridge covered all over with genuine 18s and 20s. And if I have a suspicion that my soft-hackle is in danger of actually imitating some immature form of aquatic insect, I can always get a look at the insect in question and make my decisions about hackle length on legitimate imitative grounds rather than on the airier terms of tradition and taste.

Gary Tanner, a fellow former director of the American Museum of Fly Fishing who did graduate field studies of ruffed grouse, recently read one of my complaints about the problem of finding small grouse hackles for these flies. He sent me a note: "Guess you didn't know the secret to getting small grouse feathers (18 and 20) is to set interception traps in alder runs in August and catch 3 month old chicks and steal their feathers. Been doing it for years."

Great, Gary. Thanks. Next time I'm in New England in August and just happen to have some interception traps handy, I'll take care of this. Why couldn't you just send me some feathers?

But thanks to Gary, a couple years ago I had the chance to examine some gorgeous soft-hackled flies that Ernest Schwiebert tied and donated to the museum. At the hands of one of the most influential writers and theorists in the sport's history, the soft-hackled fly fulfills its potential for a functional kind of elegance. And the deliberate variations in body and hackle from pattern to pattern, each to match a particular species of caddisfly, in no way compromise the obvious "rightness" of the proportions of this or that individual pattern. It's nice to see the soft-hackle's versatility so beautifully confirmed, even if I know I never will tie them to look that good.

If you want to sharpen your eye and focus your attention, try this: The next time you fish with soft-hackles, think of those hardy souls and cool hands who fished the same flies for upward of two thousand years with no reel and no way to lengthen or shorten the line. Aelian's angler used a rod maybe 6 feet long and line the same length. Nineteenth-century practitioners of Cutcliffe's era, still not using a reel, doubled or even tripled the length of both rod and line. If you're a typically outfitted modern fly fisher, your rod is well within that wide range of lengths, so it should work just fine.

Pull out line and leader about two feet longer than the rod. Then pull a few more inches of line from the reel and loop it around the reel seat a couple times, just to ensure that you can't get any more. Tie on a soft-hackle or two, wade into the river, and see what you can do.

CHAPTER TWELVE

Wings

One of the most charmingly contradictory notions I have come across among fly theorists is the "scissoring" wing. Cast a streamer—let's say a nice, big Light Spruce Fly—well across the current, and retrieve it with snappy jerks that cause the wing and body to alternately narrow and expand. When you are pulling hardest, the body and wing are compressed sleekly together. Then, when you let the line go slack and the fly slides back with the current, the wing can lift far off the body, achieving the scissoring effect that seems to be attractive to fish.

What makes the technique so interesting and yet bizarre, aside from the fact that it really does work, is the juicy, deep-dish pie it tosses in the face of imitative theory. On the one hand, it's easy enough to imagine a small fish behaving erratically for some reason, shooting forward and then hanging still or even drifting back with the current. But on the other hand, my readings in the natural history and folklore of North American fish haven't revealed a single fish species that can split itself open along its lateral line, from its tail almost to its mouth, and then proceed to frog through the water like that. Or is it a fish imitation at all? Crayfish do some pretty weird backward swimming, and some large insects have even stranger locomotion styles.

My first fishing book, and still among those I admire most, was Joe Brooks's great and cordial *Trout Fishing*, published in 1972, the year I took up fly fishing. I can never thank my brother Steve enough for giving it to me.

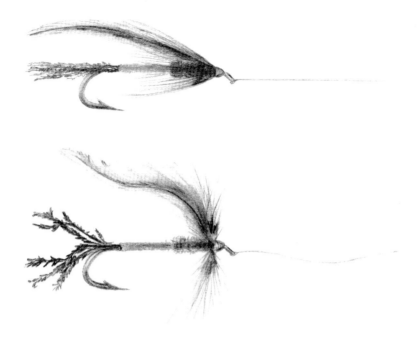

The scissoring of a streamer's wings as it is alternately pulled forward and then released to drift in the current seems to create an impression of some bizarre living creature that appeals to many trout. ILLUSTRATION BY MARSHA KARLE.

It introduced me to scissoring wings right off, with a pair of photographs, probably taken in an aquarium, showing a yellow marabou streamer achieving this wonderful effect. In the first photograph, the streamer is being pulled forward and appears streamlined. In the second, the streamer has been allowed to drop back and its wing has fluffed out away from the body, leaving a big, long gap between the two.

The enchantment of that image has never left me. For years, I resisted using matukas, feather-wing streamers with their wings lashed down along the length of the body, because of it. Sure, matukas look great, and sure, they prevent the feather from hanging up under the hook, but it's hardly an honest wing anymore when it's tied down like that. Isn't it just the top of the body now? It can't wave around where it wants or go curling way up like Dilbert's tie. How can it be attractive to the fish?

Well, setting aside the harsh reality that on a given day almost anything might be attractive to fish and the even harsher reality that matukas catch a lot of them, I'm left marveling over how long we have been unable to decide just what the wet-fly wing is supposed to do or be.

What Was the Wing?

Modern angling theorists have struggled with this question on a fundamental level, partly because we're so unsure of what all those earlier generations had in mind when they tied wet flies anyway, and we're even less sure what the trout made of such things. In *The Fly* (2001), Andrew Herd captured the strange essence of this singular lapse of reason among the fly tiers who were so devoted to the wet fly: "It is interesting to think that the arguments which raged over almost every aspect of fly design later in the nineteenth century studiously avoided the inescapable fact that winged duns are not to be found several inches under the surface, breasting the current."

Good point. That handsome wing sprouting up and over the body resembles nothing so much as the wing of a fully emerged adult mayfly, which by all rights should be floating on the surface, not zooming around a foot or two down in the water. How did that upright wing get attached to almost every great old wet-fly pattern, and why did those anglers so happily fish such an improbable thing year after year, when they could see, if they bothered to look, that the underwater forms of the flies they were supposedly imitating were usually nymphs that didn't have such wings? It's still hard for us to understand, probably because we weren't there and the writings of those fellows are just not complete enough to explain their thinking or the gap in their thinking. "In effect," Andrew concluded, "the whole elaborately constructed thesis of wet-fly fishing rested on quicksand. But no matter, fish were being caught, because trout have to take what they are given."

Over the years, anglers have come up with some pretty good excuses for this situation. Some believed that wet flies looked like drowned duns; that would certainly explain how adults got below the surface, though not, as Andrew pointed out, how they could seemingly swim along so vigorously. Others believed that wet flies looked like emerging mayflies or caddis with partly opened wings—or at least enough like those immature stages of insects to get the job done and fool the fish. Still others thought that wet flies looked like tiny fish.

I don't doubt that all these theories were and are true sometimes. Those beautifully swept-back wings could easily look like the partly exposed wing of some emerging insect, especially if the forward motion of the fly kept the wing from standing up too straight. It's easier still to imagine them resembling very small fish, especially the larger ones. But even if these effects were achieved occasionally by the traditional wet fly, we are left to wonder why more people all those years didn't seem to understand precisely what the flies they were casting imitated.

And to get right to the quick of the matter, the wet flies worked, so most anglers probably didn't worry about what they looked like.

But when wet flies stopped working so well, as happened when brown trout arrived in North America and started demanding a new reality in fly patterns, the anglers did begin to worry about it. In short order, they invented a bundle of new imitative approaches and several competing theories of how to make flies look more like real insects.

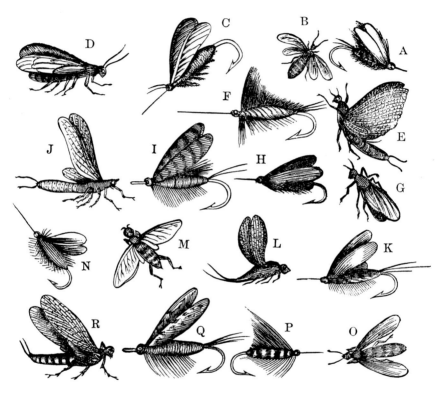

The traditional wet fly, as it was popularized and standardized in the late 1800s, remains one of the great enigmas in fly-tying theory, especially in the matter of the wings. Genio Scott's Fishing in American Waters *(1875) was typical in its puzzling portrayal of these flies. In Scott's illustration, each adult insect was paired with the artificial fly intended to imitate it (A with B, C with D, and so on). These adult insects—mayflies, stoneflies, and others—were all most commonly found either in the air or on the surface of the water, but the flies tied to imitate them were often fished wet. These artificials were successful for a variety of reasons, but angling historian Andrew Herd's whimsical conclusion that the flies caught fish because "trout have to take what they are given" is probably as good an explanation as any.*

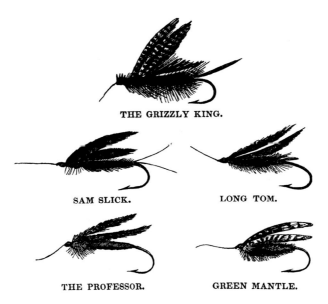

THE GRIZZLY KING.

SAM SLICK.   LONG TOM.

THE PROFESSOR.   GREEN MANTLE.

Though most fly patterns from the nineteenth century and earlier were said to imitate various insects, a surprising number of nineteenth-century wet flies were tied with elongated bodies and wings, which could have either inadvertently or intentionally imitated small fish. Among the most notable examples of these were the flies illustrated in James Wilson's The Rod and the Gun *(1844), which have the stretched proportions common among the streamers that were popular in America at the beginning of the twentieth century.*

Putting Wings to Work

Even when the old flies still worked just fine, and many do even today, some anglers were thinking about them. Some were thinking really hard and trying to make the wings as helpful as they could be. They had some interesting ideas too.

We're stuck with the paltry evidence left us in the early fishing literature to tell us how all this came about. Even the faint trail left in books and periodicals makes it clear that by 1800 or so, at least a few people were replacing the fairly stiff and unresponsive little wing on the typical wet fly with something more pliant. The leading historian of Irish fly patterns, E. J. Malone, recently responded to a question of mine about historical winging styles with this observation: "It is also a recorded fact that the old Rogan of Ballyshannon flies were tied in a meticulous fashion with all the proper ingredients on the wing (and in their proper place), and the final stage was to take a needle and separate *every fibre* in the wing so that it might move in the water."

151

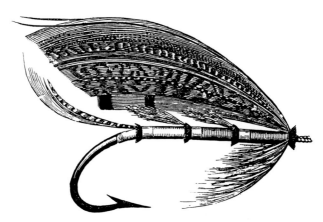

Few fly tiers among us would have the fortitude to tie a Victorian-era Atlantic salmon fly and then separate every fiber in its complex married wing with a dubbing needle, but that is precisely what some historical fly fishers did in order to ensure that the wing "breathed" properly. The pattern is a Beaconsfield, from George Kelson's The Salmon Fly: How to Dress It and How to Use It *(1895).*

Besides trying to make the wing act more alive or just act at all, it was probably inevitable that the idea of lengthening the wing would occur to some fishermen. Some may just have liked the additional liveliness a softer, longer wing gave the fly; they may not have cared what the fish thought it was.

Others, like James Wilson in *The Rod and the Gun* (1844), were intentionally meeting the definition of the modern streamer long before it was supposedly invented around 1900. Wilson wanted to imitate a small fish, and he recommended a silver-tinsel-bodied fly with wings "of a narrow elongated form, composed either of pure white or pale gray, or a mixture of both," which he said, "has a very glistening aspect in the water, looking somewhat like a small disabled fish." Sounds like any number of later crippled-minnow imitations. Similar flies are illustrated in engravings in T. C. Hofland's *The British Angler's Manual* (1839). For proportion, use of long-shanked hooks, and elongated wings, they were the equal of any modern streamer except the most extreme forms. Tie them on eyed hooks instead of those bothersome snelled ones, and I'd use them today.

Though some American writers persist in thinking of the streamer as a purely American invention, it obviously wasn't. I don't think it was unusual for nineteenth-century British fly fishers to be thinking of fish imitations. As I pointed out in *American Fly Fishing: A History* (1987), they were even using large fish imitations in salt water. Besides, they were quite aware of the behavior of little fish, with their fluid, "streaming" motions. A quick check of the *Oxford English Dictionary (OED)* indicates that the word "streamer," as applied to tinsels, ribbons, and feathers, was in use by the late 1700s or early 1800s. And the editor of the posthumous 1860 edition of John Younger's *River Angling for Salmon and Trout* added an interesting footnote to Younger's discussion of fishing with live minnows, saying, "Small minnows for trout angling are best, and they should be white-bellied. The reddish minnows, commonly called 'streamers' are not taken readily by the trouts." I have not learned who first applied the same term to an artificial fly. The *OED* cites Dixie Carroll's *Fishing Tackle and Kits* (1919) as referring to "red feather streamers" being attached to a fly, so there apparently was a period when the term "streamer" might mean either the feathers themselves or the whole fly.

But giving the wing a fishlike profile was only part of what these nineteenth-century fishermen had in mind. Through the 1800s and even more so since then, wet-fly anglers worried their way through heightening the lifelike qualities of the wing. For the purposes of this discussion, I'm going to sidestep the awkward complication that other schools of thought existed among British fishermen, including many soft-hackle enthusiasts who, by the mid-1800s, had largely discarded the wing as an unnecessary element in wet-fly design.

Atlantic salmon fishermen, whose flies became increasingly complex and elegant as the nineteenth century passed, put a lot of thought into what those exotic, multicolored, married-feather wings on salmon flies might look like to fish. William Scrope (apparently pronounced "Scroop") in *Days and Nights of Salmon Fishing in the Tweed* (1843) spoke of working his salmon fly with "short jerks" as it swung across the current because this "sets the wings in a state of alternate expansion and contraction that is extremely captivating." I suppose this even could have included some scissoring.

Achieving this sort of action became loosely known as causing the fly to breathe. Francis Francis, perhaps the foremost angling authority of the following generation, wasn't so sure it worked or that we could know for sure what the fish made of it. In *A Book on Angling* (quoting from the 1887 edition), he allowed that "some anglers, and some writers, lay great stress upon working your fly, and how you are to humour it into the stream, and make it work so that all the fibre-like pinions open and shut like a living thing, &c.; but it is all chips and porridge."

These days I don't hear a lot of people on the Firehole using the expression "chips and porridge," but I think what he meant was that giving the fly this action didn't matter much and, by implication, it's pretty hard to prove such theories anyway. Besides, it was Atlantic salmon they were

The flourishing of the craft of Atlantic salmon fly tying in the nineteenth century led to a proliferation in complex patterns with richly colored and textured wings. Even more than traditional wet flies for trout, these salmon flies have raised enduring and perplexing questions about the cognitive processes, tastes, and even sanity of the fish they caught. Detail from an oil painting, A Fly Dresser's Work Bench, *by Catherine M. Wood, c. 1890, American Museum of Fly Fishing, Manchester, Vermont (85.1.96).*

talking about, and the mystery was heightened by the salmon's famously unempirical response to flies of any kind. Francis, a man of his time, said that "salmon, like maidens, are sometimes capricious."

It's worth an aside, however, to point out that the small fish that these flies might have been imitating are as incapable of swelling up and shrinking down again and again as they are of scissoring. Breathing flies no doubt imitate something. Maybe the changing shape of the breathing artificial fly is translated into some shimmering effect as the angles of reflections from its sides change. I have often wondered whether the hackle collar on the Light Spruce Fly and similar patterns, which expands and collapses each time the fly is yanked through the water, might resemble the motions of the large pectoral fins on a sculpin. Or maybe the fish just sees this puffing and deflating thing, recognizes it as a life form it can fit into its mouth, and eats it with no regard for other elements of unrealism.

154

Losing Track of the Wing

Because of the limitations of illustration style in old fishing books, especially those magnificently colorful fly encyclopedias of the late nineteenth and early twentieth centuries, it is sometimes hard to tell what fly tiers had in mind. It's ironic that readers of fly-fishing books before about 1880 may have been getting a clearer message about how to make wings that really worked than those who read later books. Historian Ken Cameron has pointed out that an unfortunate side effect of the revolution of printing technology in the late nineteenth century, though it gave us some of our most sumptuously illustrated fly-fishing books and catalogs, was to reduce the portrayal of the flies to two simplistic dimensions. Fly illustrations became homogenized or at least standardized. A fly that had been tied by its originator with split wings or wings constructed with, say, paired duck flank feathers with their concave sides fanned out could easily become a very pretty, very flat thing at the hands of an inattentive job engraver and printer who thought he knew that all these little things looked alike from the side. After about 1900, almost all flies in fishing books were portrayed directly from the side and solely as having length and height.

Louis Rhead, who knew that natural insects vary enormously in shape, size, and proportion and whose beautifully produced *American Trout Stream Insects* (1916) tried and failed to serve as the first important American angler's entomology, saw this ignorant standardization happening and tried to fight it: "If the angler will carefully study a page or two of colored commercial flies, he will observe a continued weariness of the same cocked wings spread outward, the same shaped body, all of the same size; the only difference being in the color of the wings, body, and hackle."

But Rhead was ignored as often when he was right as when he was wrong. By the time of Ray Bergman's beloved *Trout* (1938), color printing was regularly vivid and sharp, but when you look at the flies in that book, especially at their wings, you'll see row after row, page after page, of wet flies that have nearly identical profiles, wing design, and proportions. Color is almost the only meaningful variable. You could find more differentiation of shape, proportion, and even winging method in some British books a hundred years older.

Though sometimes it's hard to tell what the fly tiers had in mind by looking at those gorgeous chromolithographs in some of the older books, it's clear they were trying a lot of things. The sort of wings we now associate almost solely with the fan-wing Royal Coachman appeared on a number of old wet flies; no doubt those cupped feathers, reaching out on both sides of the fly, did some intriguing flapping and blooshing as they were

155

pulled through a stillwater. I notice a recent growth in attention among fishing writers to the "acoustic signature" of large flies in the water; anglers 150 years ago were evidently aware of the effects of such flies in attracting gamefish.

In *Fly-Rods and Fly-Tackle* (1885), Henry Parkhurst Wells recommended tying the Yellow Professor and Grizzly King with wings "made of two separate mallard feathers, set with the concave side outward instead of in the usual manner." Wells admitted that "in the air such a fly is not attractive, but handle it by a series of short, slow jerks a little below the surface of the water, and its wings will open and shut so that it really appears to swim—a process which seems amazingly to strike the fancy of large trout."

The almost incredible variety of whole feathers that were used to wing larger wet flies must have provided anglers with quite an array of actions just because of inherent differences among the feathers in stiffness, absorption, and other qualities that would affect how they moved or didn't move. How many of these fishermen were aware of the differences or made much of them, we can't know.

But every now and then, someone would come along with a genuinely different approach. Carrie Stevens of Maine began tying flies in the early 1920s without ever having seen it done by anyone else. Being so completely unconditioned to the conventions and fashions of the "right" way to do it, she became a pioneer not only of extreme wing length, but also of a refreshingly unorthodox way of mounting the wings. Her wings, most with her trademark "shoulder" of another feather, were essentially side mounted. These long, trim feathers did not pop up like a sail above the fly's body but ran along both sides. The theory was that this style of wing mounting, if done with the right touch, allowed the water to ripple along the side of the fly and give the tail a little wag. If so, it must have been a great attractant to fish. If not, it still was a terrific fly.

Stevens's flies also provide a cautionary lesson in how hidebound we can be when it comes to fly theory. Take a look at her original flies, as pictured in the gorgeous book *Carrie Stevens: Maker of Rangeley Favorite Trout and Salmon Flies* (2000) by Graydon and Leslie Hilyard. Then for contrast, look at how her most famous fly, the Gray Ghost, is portrayed in Ray Bergman's *Trout.* Bergman's book was certainly the most influential American trout-fishing book for several decades in the mid-1900s. The artist for the Bergman book, Edgar Burke, was the opposite of Stevens; he knew all about flies and fly tying, which meant that he knew exactly how a fly was *supposed* to look. So he turned the Gray Ghost, like all the other streamers pictured in *Trout,* back into what many of us still think a streamer is: just a stretched wet fly with the wing mounted on top. The

For many years, fly tiers have experimented with a variety of wings made to diverge and rejoin, create a disturbance, or otherwise give a suggestion of life. A Light Spruce Fly tied with its wing feathers concave side in presents one appearance, and the same fly with its wing feathers concave side out presents another. The two flies exhibit considerably different behavior in the water.
ILLUSTRATION BY MARSHA KARLE.

157

Carrie Stevens's original Gray Ghost streamer, with its side-mounted wings, was a significant departure from fly styles of the time. Many later tiers, not understanding the intent of the unorthodox style, simply repositioned the wings in the conventionally proper location atop the hook, thus defeating the purpose of the pattern. ILLUSTRATION BY MARSHA KARLE.

experts thus got it wrong and entirely missed the point of Stevens's fly-tying contribution.

Today, what with a revolution in synthetic materials, the expansion of fly-fishing attention to ever more species of fish and the things they eat, and a whole world of cool hands taking on the challenges of tying new generations of wet-fly and streamer mutations, wings are made of every imaginable combination of fibers. Feathers are mounted in many places along the hook shank and in unexpected planes, even at oddly canted angles to further heighten the wobbly crippled-minnow effect that Wilson thought to achieve 160 years ago. Many artificial fibers, glowing, sparkling, rippling along like tiny currents of light, appear in modern fly wings. We may owe saltwater fly tiers the most in their inventiveness with the new fibers and new possibilities.

If there is a single unified theory of the fly wing out there, we seem to be getting farther from it rather than nearer. Unless Francis Francis was right that the only meaningful factor is the mood and inclination of each individual fish, and the rest is "all chips and porridge."

CHAPTER THIRTEEN

Skippers, Skaters, Dappers, and Dancers

I recently spent two days floating Wyoming's Snake River with several skilled, well-traveled fishermen. Of all the interesting things I saw them do, none was quite so entertaining as the action they imparted to big floating flies. Over the course of sixteen hours of fishing, I'm sure that the majority of our casts involved slapping those flies onto the water right along the bank, then skipping, popping, or otherwise dragging them in some way. Sometimes we'd haul back hard enough to submerge the fly for a second, wait for it to pop back to the surface, and then do it again, just as bass fishermen have done for many years. A lot of fish approved.

A few weeks later, I revisited a steelhead river I'd last fished twenty-eight years earlier. I was startled to see my tradition-steeped friends there doing essentially the same thing. I had left them alone for a mere generation, and they'd devolved from using elegant greased-line techniques to dragging rudely constructed muddlers up, down, and across the surface.

For a history-minded fisherman, this was great stuff. Not that long ago, such treatment of dry flies was nearly sacrilegious in proper fly-fishing society. Except for a few rarefied situations, such as when fishing a riffling hitch for Atlantic salmon, fly-fishing orthodoxy insisted that a surface fly that did anything but float quietly was a sign of incompetence and doomed to fail.

I've already suggested that the formal dry-fly code popularized by Frederic Halford and his admirers in late-1800s England was in fact a pretty restrictive prescription. But a lot of people liked it and for good rea-

159

The foam-board fly holder on a modern western drift boat suggests the extent to which the traditional dead drift dry fly has been replaced on big rivers by high-buoyancy, bass-buggy attractor patterns durable enough to be popped, slammed, and dragged across the surface of the river for hours.

son. Keeping a dry fly from dragging is challenging, and fishing such a fly through a perfectly undisturbed drift is satisfying work.

But the purists were missing out on a lot of fun. When Leonard Wright published his thoughtful *Fishing the Dry Fly as a Living Insect* (1972), a whole generation of anglers were ready for a breath of fresh iconoclasm. Wright's fluttering caddis patterns, tied to slide easily over the surface and twitched lightly at strategic moments, provided it.

But Wright's recommendations were just the latest in a long and surprisingly diverse set of methods, some dating back centuries, by which anglers have tried to attract trout to the surface with an active rather than passive fly.

Hovering

Wright acknowledged the inspiration he had gotten from one of those methods. While still a young angler in the Adirondacks in the 1940s, veteran locals outfished him with three-fly rigs of vintage wet flies. They'd hang this rig a short distance off the back of a slowly moving boat, let the

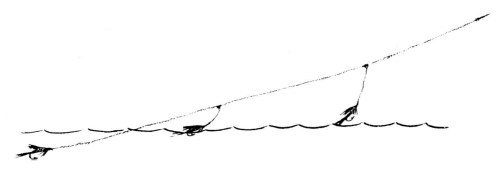

Fred Everett, in Fun with Trout: Trout Fishing in Words, Paint & Lines *(1952), showed the basic three-fly rig for using the tail fly as an anchor so that a dropper could be suspended above the surface.*

first two flies sink, and keep the highest fly suspended over the surface, bouncing it up and down like a low-flying insect. In 1914, the American dry-fly pioneer George LaBranche said that the bouncing dropper usually just served to attract the fish, which then took the sunken fly or flies. In *Fun with Trout* (1952), Fred Everett recommended keeping the tail fly under the water, a first dropper fly swimming around on the surface, and a second dropper dancing up and down above the water.

Done either by a wading fisherman or from a boat, the technique has been described in print by pretty much every generation of American anglers back to at least 1840. But it's hardly the oldest technique for bringing artificial flies to life on the surface of a stream.

Dapping

The oldest known techniques for giving a fly the semblance of life and motion date from the time when fly fishing was about as likely to mean using a real insect for bait as using an artificial fly. For the first several centuries after fly fishing emerged from its long anonymity of practice and became the subject of written tracts—let's say from the 1200s until the 1800s—fly lines lacked the weight needed for casting very far or forcefully. Fly fishers were much more at the mercy of the wind than we are today.

But being resourceful, they worked at putting the wind to use in a technique known as dapping. It involved the use of a blow-line, which had nothing to do with cocaine but everything to do with the light and easily airborne fly lines in use at the time. In a technique probably as old as fly fishing, some of our earliest writers put the wind to use to move the fly where they wanted it. Juan de Bergara, in the Spanish document now known as *The Astorga Manuscript* (1624), said the March winds heralded "great sport," apparently because they enabled blow-line fishing with artificial flies. Charles Cotton, in his masterful fly-fishing instructions in the 1676 edition of Izaak Walton's *Compleat Angler,* gave us this advice:

> And this way of fishing we call daping, dabbing, or dibbing; wherein you are always to have your line flying before you up or down the river, as the wind serves, and to angle as near as you can to the bank of the same side whereon you stand, though where you see a fish rise near you, you may guide your quick fly over him, whether in the middle, or on the contrary side; and if you are pretty well out of sight, either by kneeling or the interposition of a bank, or bush, you may almost be sure to raise, and take him too, if it be presently done.

Among other things, this meant that in order to fish with the wind at your back, you cast upstream, across stream, or downstream, as you could. You were at the mercy of the wind, but if you knew how to put the wind to work, the trout were often at the mercy of you.

In 1676, Charles Cotton offered anglers his immortal admonition to fish "fine and far off" for trout. This was achieved for the next couple centuries by means of 12- to 20-foot rods with no reels and lines the same length as the rods. The length of these rods greatly facilitated the variety of practices known as dapping and blow-line fishing. Engraving of Denham, *on the Colne River, England, from Sir Humphrey Davy's* Salmonia *(1828).* HAND COLORED BY MARSHA KARLE.

I think it especially interesting that this is to a great extent a fly-fishing technique we have lost. I hear of it infrequently except as it has descended to us as a technique for lake fishing in the United Kingdom.

One reason we don't do it much is that our tackle has been "improved" out of the ability of doing it. The rods of Cotton's time, from 15 to 18 feet in length, would have been ideal for dapping; rods of that length sound to us like real barge poles, but he claimed they could be constructed lightly enough to be used with one hand. Trout fishers didn't use reels in Cotton's time, so the line would have been attached to the tip of the rod, which meant that the angler couldn't handle a line much longer than the rod and often used a line much shorter. For fishing with natural flies—that is, real insects impaled on hooks—Cotton recommended a line about half the length of the rod. For fishing with artificial flies, he preferred a "line longer by a yard and a half, or sometimes two yards, than your rod."

These dimensions—say an 18-foot rod with a 22-foot line—go a long way toward clarifying two of Cotton's most famous admonitions. The first, so often quoted these days, was that you fish "fine, and far off." Today that has come to mean spiderweb-fine leaders fished with herculean casts of great length and precision. It's hard to imagine a modern expert fly fisher regarding any cast of less than sixty or even seventy feet as meeting that definition. What Cotton meant was indeed fine and far off by the standards of his day, but it involved the fixed maximum length of rod and line. With no reel and the line firmly attached to the end of the rod, no line could be shot to extend the cast, and it all was done in the presence of the wind. In Cotton's own words, you "cast your fly to the utmost length of your rod and line, up or down the river, as the gale serves."

And there was no problem with those awkward moments when you tried to land a fish at the end of a line so much longer than your rod. As Cotton saw it, "Every one that can afford to angle for pleasure, has somebody to do for him." In other words, some neighborhood boy you'd hired for the day was responsible for landing your fish anyway.

The second endlessly invoked remark by Cotton established what we still regard as an impressive statement about an angler's skill at handling the horsehair lines of the day. The lines were tapered to a point, from many strands of horsehair at the butt to very few at the tip. Cotton said that no more than two hairs were necessary in the final segment that connected to the fly. He exhorted fly fishers that "he that cannot kill a trout of twenty inches long with two, in a river clear of wood and weeds, as this [river] and some others of ours are, deserves not the name of angler." It is taking nothing away from the standard of skill Cotton was prescribing to notice that an 18-foot rod, soft and resilient as it would be, would give the fly fisher a great abundance of patient leverage for just this kind of work, especially in water clear of obstructions.

Dapping would have been much easier with Cotton's tackle than with our modern lines, which are engineered for longer casts and lack the ready air buoyancy of ancient horsehair and grass lines, much less the fine silk floss lines used in the 1800s for blow-lining. At least in my experience, the winds it takes to loft a reasonable length of even a modern 4-weight line are necessarily strong enough to make it difficult to bring the fly down with the kind of accuracy that Cotton apparently achieved with horsehair. If I were to go out today with the intention of blow-line fishing, say on a day with a good "grasshopper wind," I'd probably wish for a 1- or 2-weight line and a nice, long rod to lift it well into the breeze.

Bobbing and Swimming

But dapping, even three hundred years ago, applied to other meanings and practices that still do work today. Walton talked about the simplest form of dapping and added some more variants to the term. After describing the various natural insects that were available for the technique, he explained it as follows:

> With these and a short line (as I showed, to angle for a chub), you may dape or dop, and also with a grasshopper, behind a tree, or in any deep hole; still making it to move on the top of the water, as if it were alive, and still keeping yourself out of sight, you shall certainly have sport if there be trouts; yea, in a hot day, but especially in the evening of a hot day, you will have sport.

When John Brown published his *American Angler's Guide* (1845), he included about eleven pages on the techniques of fly-fishing for trout. As was common in those first American books on fishing, almost all of his information was cribbed or quoted from contemporary British books. Brown seemed to know something about fly fishing but slavishly deferred to other writers, probably out of laziness but maybe also out of respect. What I find especially revealing in Brown's selection of topics is that about 40 percent of his fly-fishing text was devoted to dapping, repeating what Cotton, T. C. Hofland in *The British Angler's Manual* (1839), and others had written about it.

That so much attention was paid to noncasting aspects of fly fishing 150 years ago suggests how little about presentation had changed in the previous 150 years and how much has changed since. Brown's extended consideration of dapping, which he called "bush fishing" for the neces-

The simplest form of dapping, simply hanging a fly over the bank and perhaps bouncing it up and down on the surface, was illustrated by Thomas Bewick in 1847. Even this small an image gave the imaginative Bewick, an enthusiastic angler, room to tell a bit of a story. The branches suspended above the current no doubt hosted insects that carelessly fell into the water but probably sheltered the spot from most conventional casts. Dapping was perhaps the only way to reach the spot. HAND COLORED BY MARSHA KARLE.

sity of hiding behind the shrubbery to get close enough to dangle your fly over the water, tells us that it has been only fairly recently in the two-millennia-plus history of fly fishing that we became so focused on casting as an essential and constant element of the sport. With equipment that couldn't reach very far, you naturally spent more time stalking, crouching, and dapping.

This short form of dapping doesn't make it into a lot of the modern fishing technique books, probably because it doesn't require any fly line except the leader but perhaps also because it is more than vaguely like bait fishing. Besides, it is such an intuitive practice that many of us can remember inventing it ourselves. Sometime early in your fishing career, you saw a trout rising tight against a bank or under some brush and simply crept up low and close enough to simply lower a fly, hanging from the rod's tip-top by a few feet of tippet, onto the water. Maybe, following Walton, you gave the fly a little action by bouncing it up and down or swinging it from side to side. In the mid-1970s, I witnessed my brother Steve invent streamer dapping, easing a bucktail into a curl of water among half-submerged tree roots on the lower Au Sable in Michigan; the brown he caught wasn't all that big, but it was the day's only fish worth remembering.

By the way, Colonial Americans have been given credit for practicing a version of dapping in the Southeast in the 1760s. The naturalist William Bartram described locals fishing for bass from a canoe; in my book *American Fly Fishing: A History,* I mistakenly said he observed Indians doing this, but it was whites. Using a heavy pole 10 or 12 feet in length and a line about 20 inches long, they swung a heavy "bob" constructed from "three large hooks, back to back. These are fixed very securely, and covered with the white hair of a deer's tail, shreds of a red garter, and some particoloured feathers, all of which form a tuft, or tassel, nearly as large as one's fist, and entirely cover and conceal the hooks." This arrangement was then swung over the surface, sometimes touching the water, until the fish came up and grabbed it. Bartram called it a trout, but presumably he was talking about largemouth bass.

Some writers have said that this Bartram account was an early example of dapping in America, but I'm still not sure. The equipment described was so different from the far lighter tackle of dapping as defined and used at the time that it's difficult to consider it fly fishing, but it would be nice to know whether the anglers were inspired by British fly-fishing techniques of the day. By the 1840s, some British anglers were using flies about as large as these bobs to take saltwater fish, and many modern fly fishers use flies this size to take tarpon or marlin, so who's to say what's a fair definition of dapping?

Slapping

Modern fly fishers have popularized a dramatic new version of the key element of dapping, the arrival of the fly on the surface of the water. Though no region can take credit for developing these techniques, I suppose I learned about them from Charles Brooks's books, especially my favorite, *The Trout and the Stream* (1974), in which Charlie provided newcomers to the West with a nice summary of the techniques and gear that were being developed for western streams. In contrast to the advice normally given to dry-fly fishers, emphasizing the need for a quiet presentation to avoid spooking the fish, he stressed the importance of accurately imitating the way a big fly arrived, because it often attracted attentive trout just by landing.

So Charlie encouraged fishermen to slam big floating flies down on the water with a "juicy splash" in keeping with the impact of large grasshoppers, salmon flies, and other sizable insects. This has long been a common approach when fishing big, rubber-legged floating monstrosities from drift boats. It was a nice lesson in imitation. He also reported on the

A steeply undercut bank on a small spring creek invites the juicy splash of a large dry fly to entice the trout from shelter.

equally unorthodox tactic of casting a hopper or deer-hair mouse into the grass overhanging the stream, then gently pulling it free in imitation of some careless insect falling into the water. He further described watching a large brown trout actually jump up to hit the grass and dislodge grasshoppers. Surface feeding indeed.

Fluttering

In the 1800s, the development of the split-cane fly rods and silk fly lines that have largely been credited with turning fly *fishers* more exclusively into fly *casters* did nothing to lessen our interest in making flies do attractive things on the surface of the water. But I think creative anglers were always onto this. Hewett Wheatley, in *The Rod and Line* (1849), introduced several moth imitations, all tied with whole-feather wings, from guinea hen, pheasant, or owl. He recommended a special trick for fishing them

167

In 1886, Wakeman Holberton patented and promoted his Fluttering Fly. No slouch at commercial overstatement, Holberton described these flies as "the greatest and most radical improvement in fishing tackle ever made." He said his reverse-tied flies could be pulled across the surface of the water with "a lifelike and fluttering motion." ILLUSTRATION BY MARSHA KARLE.

when they were first cast and still floating on the water's surface: "Add a tremulous motion of the wrist, and you will communicate that fluttering movement on the surface of the water, which is peculiarly attractive."

In 1886, angling writer Wakeman Holberton took out a patent on his "fluttering fly," which was a reverse-tied pattern with the wings and hackle both slanting back from bend of the hook toward the eye. Apparently the idea was that as you drew this pattern across the surface, the wings and hackle would expand a little, or "flutter" and, as one observer put it, "seam the surface with an attractive wake."

Bouncing

It seems clear that giving a floating fly a little action now and then was popular long before George LaBranche, in *The Dry Fly and Fast Water* (1914), proposed his "bounce cast," also called the "fluttering cast." As I understand it, LaBranche intended this rather obscurely described technique to improve on the jerk by causing the fly, on a short cast in which it was to touch the water first, to land on the water for only an instant before lifting and coming down again. I've never actually seen this done as he described it, and as I've never done it accidentally in more than thirty years of haphazard and marginally competent casting, I doubt I could do it on purpose. But it is regarded as a milestone in American dry-fly writing, so I'd better let you hear his version of it:

> This cast is supposed to represent the action of the fluttering insect, the fly merely alighting upon the water, rising, alighting again, repeating the movement three or four times at most; finally coming to rest and being allowed to float down-stream. It rarely comes off, but when

it does it is deadly; and for the good of the sport, I am glad that it is difficult, though sorry, too, for the pleasure of accomplishing it successfully is really greater than that of taking fish with it. The cast is made with a very short line—never over twenty-five feet—and the fly alone touches the water. The action of the fly is very similar to that produced by the method known as "dapping," but instead of being merely dangled from the rod, as is the case when "dapping," the fly is actually cast. It should be permitted to float as far as it will after its fluttering or skipping has ceased. The beginner practising the cast will do well to cast at right angles to the current, and he should choose rather fast water for his experimenting. The speed of the water will cause the fly to jump, and the action it should have will be the more readily stimulated than if the first attempts are made on slow water.

And here is how one of our great modern fly theorists, the late Gary LaFontaine, interpreted this same passage. This appears in a most helpful chapter on dry-fly motion, entitled "Unnatural Acts," in Gary's book *The Dry Fly* (1994). He called it the tick cast:

> The "tick," devised by George LaBranche and called the "bounce cast" in *The Dry Fly and Fast Water*, works splendidly in certain water types. The name bounce cast is inaccurate, though, because the fly is not bouncing and landing but is barely touching the surface. The trick is to let the artificial tick the water in a series of false casts. These touches, all at the same spot, send splashes of light under the meniscus. The meniscus is silver from reflected light—tap on it and that lights sparks. The tactic works best if the fly doesn't break through the surface film.

In case the word puzzled you, I think Gary is using "meniscus" to mean the underside of the very top of the water, which has a mirrorlike appearance from underneath except in the relatively small field of vision known as the trout's window (see pages 77–79).

Disturbing the Mirror

Gary also believed that moving or twitching a dry fly was more likely to be successful if it was twitched where it would disturb the water outside or right along the edge of the trout's window. In other words, if the fly disturbed the mirror, it would be more attractive than if it was plainly visible to the trout and just disturbed clear water. Exactly how the angler was to determine where the edge of a submerged trout's window was in order to place a fly there is unclear in Gary's text, but I don't for a second doubt that he could do it.

And in recommending it, he was unknowingly echoing a sentiment expressed by one of fly fishing's earlier authorities, Alvin "Bus" Grove, whose *Lure and Lore of Fly Fishing* (1951) deserves a good deal more attention than it gets today. In a little essay entitled "A Miscellaneous Assortment of This and That," which wasn't published until recently, Bus also wrote of the great importance of the mirror in dry-fly fishing:

> You have no doubt noticed that while I indirectly referred to the trout's window, I haven't said much about it. As a matter of fact, I think from the trout's point of view, the mirror may be more important. I think most of the trout we catch with surface flies is *[sic]* the result of stimuli and recognition of light patterns outside the window.

Trying to understand how the mirror is affected by flies as they drift toward the trout has been one of the great quests of dry-fly theorists. Gary and Bus remind us that the question matters just as much to the fisherman who is purposely moving a fly as it does to the fisherman who is doing all he can to avoid any such drag. They suggest that we think about what's happening out there on the stream when we begin popping and twitching a fly across the surface. I have always tended to see the fly in terms of how much it might look, from my angle at least, like a real insect bouncing around out there. It might be a lot more useful to try to imagine what that fly is doing to crease or otherwise disturb the mirror. Unless the fly just happens to scoot across the trout's window, the disturbance of the mirror is all that the trout is seeing, after all. The disturbance of the mirror—and whatever portion of the fly protrudes through the mirror as it floats along on the surface—is all that the rising trout can see as the fly drifts toward them from upstream.

Scientists who specialize in the study of the water-air interface emphasize the extreme complexity and variability of surface films. The term as it is most often used in fishing writing means simply the fine uppermost layer of water whose surface tension buoys up our dry flies. But the surface film is actually an accumulation of inorganic matter and life that is mixed in with the water and contributes to its behavior and biological prospects. It does what we need it to, so we don't pay much attention to it, but as with the trout itself, we find that there is more there the harder we look. For example, Thomas Grubb in *The Mind of the Trout* (2003) points to several possible factors involving the surface film that may affect the trout. He reports on one study that suggests that floating mayflies may be able to sense the odors of trout through that top layer of water. The surface film carries a complicated load.

Skipping

We also owe Gary LaFontaine for a nice summary of what he called skip casting, which a lot of people do without bothering to name it. His skip cast, described in *The Dry Fly,* involves casting a fly very low over the water so that it approaches the water at nearly parallel, causing it to skip like a stone when it hits the surface and thus land more than once. (When I first read LaBranche's description of his bounce cast, I thought that this was what he was trying to say.) Because the fly travels its last few inches or feet right above the surface of the water, skipping a fly is a handy way to get it back under vegetation that overhangs the water from the streambank.

Skating

A much more ambitious departure from orthodoxy appeared in 1948, when Edward Hewitt introduced what he jokingly referred to as "butterfly fishing" in *A Trout and Salmon Fisherman for Seventy-Five Years.* The Hewitt skater was just a pair of oversize hackles wrapped facing each other, dull sides in. Once wrapped, the tier pinched the hackle turns tightly onto a short portion of the hook shank, creating a single sharp edge around their outer perimeter. It was a nuisance to cast, but Hewitt and later writers agreed that a skilled angler could give the line a little tug, lift the fly up onto that fine outer edge, and skate it for considerable distances.

Over time, techniques as diverse as these tend to mutate, and countless local practices come and go. Some fishermen friends on the Battenkill in the early 1980s, inspired by both Wright and Hewitt, trimmed the sharp hackle tips off unwinged but well-hackled small dry flies, producing a densely spiky, bottle-brush effect. They drag-skated these flies slowly, with occasional upstream pulls, across long, smooth slicks at the tails of pools, rising fish in water that seemed much too clear and shallow to be worth the bother.

The most simple version of skating is the one we generally seek to avoid: when a dry fly drags away from the preferred course of its downstream drift. Many of us, however, have had occasional if inadvertent success with such drag, when our dragging fly, trailing its embarrassing little wake across some quiet pool, was grabbed by a trout.

And again my brother Steve, ever alert for formalisms to lampoon, once announced to me his development of a new technique, "absentmindedly trolling an Adams," which involved letting his dragging fly complete its swing and then allowing it to skate and jump around on the end of the line directly downstream for a while. Meanwhile, he looked through his fly box or daydreamed until he more or less forgot about the fly. Inattention, he cynically but accurately claimed, was often the best way to get a fish to strike.

Crossing the Line

My favorite of all these techniques is both the weirdest and the most clever. It was called "cross-lining," and I understand it has been formally declared illegal on some British waters. I leave it to the armchair philosophers to decide whether it's even fly fishing. Let's hear about it from an early enthusiast, Giles Jacob, writing in *The Compleat Sportsman* (1718):

> Two persons, each being furnished with a long rod, go out together; when they come to the river they propose to fish, they separate one on one side of the water, and the other on the other side; then having a strong hair-line, in length twice the breadth of the river, one of the anglers is to fix one end of it to his rod, and by fixing a lead-plummet to the other end, throw it over to his companion, who likewise fastens that end to his rod, taking off the plummet; to this long line are fastened two short ones with hooks, the lines not exceeding two or three yards in length.

Once you and your accomplice had the line strung across the stream, you could attach any number of droppers to it and march upstream in step, creating your own hatch and hoovering up the trout. David Webster, in *The Angler and the Loop-Rod* (1885), said that the practice, which he called "double-rod fishing," was "in vogue many years ago" and involved the use of as many as forty or fifty hooks. He also said that during a good emergence of a known fly, anglers attached the appropriate artificial to every dropper, sweeping the river with one fly pattern.

Andrew Herd, who alerted me to the Jacob account, said that "although many regarded it as little more than poaching, there is no doubt that it was an enjoyable and killing method, and huge bags could be made, so it took a long while to die out."

I doubt its legitimacy too, but I agree that it must have been fun. In fact, if I could somehow give my ethics the day off, it sounds like a hoot. I can picture doing it on the lower Madison, with big deer-hair hoppers suspended on stout tippets over some of those unreachable midriver riffles. Swinging them all upstream, letting them land with a splash and float down a few feet, and then doing it again would have to work.

I also doubt that Andrew has to worry that it will die out. It's one of those marginal yet inventive little sidestreams in fly fishing into which exasperated fishermen will wander occasionally as long as there are unreachable rising trout. In *Trout Magic* (1974), the late Robert Traver left us the tale of the "dancing fly." Two of his friends, perplexed by the bouncy flight of a local insect on a pond, reinvented cross-lining, raising and lowering their two fly rods in unison to dance the artificial over the water between them. According to Traver, one of them explained that he came up with the idea after deciding that hanging the fly down over the water from a balloon would be too awkward.

CHAPTER FOURTEEN

Antidotes to Madness

In another of his books, *Trout Madness* (1960), Robert Traver seemed determined to keep us from going off fly fishing's deep end when he talked about all the unknown factors we face as we try to understand what goes on in a trout stream: "I realize I'm drifting boldly into the realm of fish mysticism, but I further suspect that usually these unknown factors embrace a good part of the entire fishing alphabet. There is so incredibly much that all men, let alone we little fishermen, don't know and perhaps can't ever know."

I am somewhat suspicious of the concept of progress as we so freely apply it to fly fishing, especially every time we reinvent some theory or add yet another "essential" fly pattern to the hundreds of previous ones I already have stuffed in my vest.

I'm all for digging deeply into the practical questions that fly fishing compels us to face. It's just that if we're not careful, we'll actually start believing our own advertising and presume not only that all those questions can be answered, but also that they must be answered. At that point, we've achieved the sad state described in 1847 by the Reverend George Washington Bethune, one of America's original and best fly-fishing theorists and commentators, while discussing the debates over exact imitation theory: "In fact, almost every practised fly-fisher has a creed and system of his own, though the advocates of exact imitation speak with artistic contempt of all who differ from them; and are in their turn ridiculed as pedantic pretenders, or mad with too much learning."

The madness of too much learning can best be avoided, I think, by admitting, as Robert Traver did even in the throes of his own trout madness, that there are more puzzles out there than we will ever be able to solve and that we're better off for that uncertainty. Traver, who showed every sign of wanting to get better at catching fish, also went right ahead and embraced the mystery, at least to the extent that it provided a valuable antidote to the obsession with becoming a perfect angler.

There is something decidedly antiauthority in Traver's view. It seems not only to go against the commercial fashions of the sport, which have always presented perfection as something you could in good part purchase, but also to be implicitly disrespectful of those hardworking souls who have become the sport's most technically proficient fish catchers. Traver, quite famously, didn't react well to the pronouncements of some of our leading experts, whom he called "trout swamis." He said they "are often highly intelligent men, perhaps lacking only in the saving perspective offered by a sense of humility and humor, whose pretensions after all cause little harm and possibly save quite a few trout. In a sense they are victims of their own hobbies." Whether we agree with him about the sport's hard-driving heroes, Traver made a good point. We want to get better at this, but maybe we don't want to turn it into the same kind of overachieving rat race we've turned everything else into.

When I told Andrew Herd that I was working on a book about trout rises and fly theory, he immediately sent me a fiery e-mail diatribe about how satisfying it would be to him if I would go after all the half-baked thinking among the great angling writers, especially the British ones. He came to rest, rhetorically, on Frederic Halford and his famous admonition that a properly fished dry fly must and will sit properly "cocked" on the water.

We've all seen this particular dry-fly truism illustrated many times. A good traditional dry fly, say a Quill Gordon or a Light Cahill, is portrayed—usually in a drawing rather than a photograph—riding high above the surface of the water, daintily supported on the steely points of its hackle and tail. You may even have made this happen by taking a new dry fly and carefully setting it down in a glass of water, where it floats just as advertised.

But as Andrew points out, that hardly ever happens out on the stream. Halford's "cocked" dry fly, the very foundation of his whole code of fly fishing, was largely imaginary. Quickly, if not immediately, even the best of these flies—false-cast into disarray, matted with floatant, and attached to a leader—flops down and comes to rest with its hook shank right on the water. Half of the hackles are submerged, steely points and all, as is the hook's bend and maybe even the tail. Get someone to cast one of those beautiful dry flies so that it drifts past you a few times and you can get a good look. It's an "emperor's new clothes" situation, in which we have been taught what is happening and have learned it so well that either we never take a good look or we do look but don't believe our eyes or else assume the failing is somehow ours.

Fred Everett's entertaining Fun with Trout *(1952), in keeping with traditional Halfordian dry-fly theory and common knowledge among generations of fly fishers, portrayed dry flies floating high on their hackle tips. After being treated with floatant and cast a few times, dry flies virtually never float this high, but as we cast, we enjoy imagining them in such jaunty, picture-perfect obedience to tradition.*

177

So there we are. Not only are there all those things that Robert Traver says we shall never know, but there also seem to be other things that we just don't want to know or aren't yet ready to know. This may not seem all that promising a stance from which to launch our little inquiries into trout-fishing theory, but it has without question yielded lots of interesting results over the past few centuries. Whether Halford was right about how his dry flies worked, he was right that they did work, and that, I suppose, will always be about the most trustworthy measure of progress we can hope for. With typical wisdom, the late Roderick Haig-Brown captured the essence of the fly-fishing problems that exasperate and inspire us, generation after generation, when he said in *Fisherman's Fall* (1964) that "one does not so much solve them as come to terms with them."

BIBLIOGRAPHY

I n the following reference list, I have included a few scientific titles that are not mentioned or referred to in the text. Most are additional publications by researchers whose other papers I have specifically mentioned. In the case of some of the more obscure and earlier fishing books, I have included reprint editions.

Ælianus, Claudius. *On the Characteristics of Animals.* Translated by A. F. Schofield. 3 vols. Cambridge, MA: Loeb Classical Library, 1958–59.

Anonymous (probably George Bird Grinnell). "The Strike in Fly-Fishing." *Forest and Stream* (February 20, 1890): 203–205.

Atherton, John. *The Fly and the Fish.* New York: McMillan, 1951.

Bachman, Robert. "Foraging Behavior of Free-Ranging Wild and Hatchery Brown Trout In A Stream." *Transactions of the American Fisheries Society* 113, no. 1 (January 1984): 1–32.

———. "How Trout Feed." *Trout* (Winter 1985): 10–16.

Bainbridge, George. *The Fly Fisher's Guide.* Liverpool, 1816. Reprint, n.p.: Flyfisher's Classic Library, 1992.

Bannon, E., and N. Ringler. "Optimum Prey Size for Stream Resident Brown Trout *(Salmon trutta):* Tests of Predictive Models." *Canadian Journal of Zoology* 64 (1986): 704–13.

Behnke, Robert. "How a Trout Sees." *Trout* (Summer 1987): 32–39.

———. *Trout and Salmon of North America.* New York: Simon & Schuster, 2002.

Bergman, Ray. *Trout.* New York: Penn Publishing, 1938.

Blacker, William. *Blacker's Art of Fly Making.* London, 1855. Reprint, n.p.: Derrydale Press, 1993.

Borger, Gary. *Nymphing: A Basic Book.* Harrisburg, PA: Stackpole Books, 1979.

———. "The Acoustic Footprint." *Fly Fisherman* (July, 2004): 44–47, 67.

Brooks, Charles. *The Trout and the Stream.* New York: Crown Publishers, 1974.

Brooks, Joe. *Trout Fishing.* New York: Harper & Row, 1972.

Brown, John. *American Angler's Guide.* New York: Burgess, Stringer, 1845.

Bryan, James E., and P. A. Larkin. "Food Specialization by Individual Trout." *Journal of the Fisheries Research Board of Canada* 29 (1972): 1615–24.

Burks, Barnard De Witt. *The Mayflies, or Ephemeroptera, of Illinois.* Bulletin of the Illinois Natural History Survey Division 26, no. 1 (May, 1953). Reprinted, Los Angeles: Entomological Reprint Specialists, 1975.

Byrnes, Gordon. "How Trout See." *Fly Fisherman* (July 1990): 56–61.

Cameron, Ken. "Fly Styles." *American Fly Fisher* (Winter 1981): 2–7.

Camp, Samuel. *Fishing with Floating Flies.* New York: Outing Publishing Company, 1913.

Carroll, Dixie. *Fishing Tackle and Kits.* Cincinnati: Stewart Kidd, 1919.

Clarke, Brian, and John Goddard. *The Trout and the Fly.* New York: Nick Lyons Books, 1980.

Connett, Eugene, III. *My Friend the Trout.* New York: D. Van Nostrand, 1961. Reprint, Stone Harbor, NJ: Meadow Run Press, 1991.

Coston, H. E. Towner. *Beneath the Surface: The Cycle of River Life.* London: Charles Scribner's Sons, 1938.

———. *Water Symphony: Fishing with a Camera.* London: Eyre and Spottiswoode, 1948.

Cutcliffe, H. C. *The Art of Trout Fishing on Rapid Streams.* South Moulton, England: Tucker Printer Square, 1863.

Davy, Sir Humphrey. *Salmonia.* London: Murray, 1828.

de Bergara, Juan. *El Manuscrito de Astorga* [The Astorga Manuscript]. Denmark: Bullanders Bogtrykkeri a·s, Skjern, Flyleaves, 1984 (modern edition/transcription).

Dukas, R., and S. Ellner. "Information Processing and Prey Detection." *Ecology* 74, no. 5 (1993): 1337–46.

Dunne, J. W. *Sunshine and the Dry Fly.* London: Black, 1924.

Edmonds, Harfield, and Norman Lee. *Brook and River Trouting.* Yorkshire: privately printed, 1916.

Eiseley, Loren. *The Immense Journey.* New York: Random House, 1957.

Everett, Fred. *Fun with Trout: Trout Fishing in Words, Paint & Lines.* Harrisburg, PA: Stackpole Books, 1952.

Felizatto, T. "Fishing 'Alla Valsesiana': Living Angling History from the Mountains of Northern Italy." *American Fly Fisher* 5, no. 8 (1978): 10–11.

Fogg, Roger. *A Handbook of North Country Trout Flies.* Congleton, England: Old Vicarage Publications, 1988.

Francis, Francis. *A Book on Angling.* London: Herbert Jenkins, 1867. Revised 6th ed., 1887. Reprint, Lyon, MS: Derrydale Press, 1993.

Gierach, John. *Good Flies.* New York: Lyons Press, 2000.

Gill, Emlyn. *Practical Dry-Fly Fishing.* New York: Scribner's, 1912.

Gordon, Sid. *How to Fish from Top to Bottom.* Harrisburg, PA: Stackpole Books, 1955.

Grove, Alvin. *The Lure and Lore of Fly Fishing.* Harrisburg, PA: Stackpole Books, 1951.

———. "A Miscellaneous Assortment of This and That." In *Limestone Legends,* compiled by Norm Shires and Jim Gilford, 245–46. Mechanicsburg, PA: Stackpole Books, 1997.

Grubb, Thomas. *The Mind of the Trout: A Cognitive Ecology for Biologists and Anglers.* Madison: University of Wisconsin Press, 2003.

Haig-Brown, Roderick. *Fisherman's Fall.* New York: Morrow, 1964.

———. *A Primer of Fly Fishing.* New York: Morrow, 1964.

Halford, Frederic. *Dry-Fly Fishing, Theory and Practice.* London: Vinton, 1889.

——— *Floating Flies and How to Dress Them.* London: Low, 1886.

Harding, Col. E. W. *The Flyfisher & the Trout's Point of View.* London: Seeley, Service, 1931.

Henderson, M. A., and T. G. Northcote. "Visual Prey Detection and Foraging in Sympatric Cutthroat Trout *(Salmo clarki clarki)* and Dolly Varden *(Salvelinus malma)." Canadian Journal of Aquatic Science* 42 (1985): 785–90.

Herd, Andrew. *The Fly.* Ellesmere, Shropshire: Medlar Press, 2001.

Hewitt, Edward Ringwood. *A Trout and Salmon Fisherman for Seventy-five Years.* New York: Charles Scribner's Sons, 1948.

Hills, John Waller. *A History of Fly Fishing for Trout.* London: Allan, 1921.

Hilyard, Graydon, and Leslie Hilyard. *Carrie Stevens: Maker of Rangeley Favorite Trout and Salmon Flies.* Mechanicsburg, PA: Stackpole Books, 2000.

Hoffmann, Richard. "A New Treatise on the Treatyse." *American Fly Fisher* 9, no. 3 (1982): 2–6.

Hofland, T. C. *The British Angler's Manual.* London: How and Parsons, 1839.

Jackson, John. *The Practical Fly-Fisher.* London: Farlow, 1854.

Jacob, Giles. *The Compleat Sportsman.* London, 1718.

Judy, John. *Slack Line Strategies for Fly Fishing.* Harrisburg, PA: Stackpole Books, 1994.

Kelson, George. *The Salmon Fly: How to Dress It and How to Use It.* London: Wymans, 1895.

Kreh, Lefty. *Fly Casting with Lefty Kreh.* Philadelphia: Lippincott, 1974.

LaBranche, George M. L. *The Dry Fly and Fast Water.* New York: Scribner's, 1914.

LaFontaine, Gary. *The Dry Fly: New Angles.* Helena, MT: Graycliff, 1994.

Lawrence, E. Simon. "Evidence for Search Image in Blackbirds, *Turdus merula* L.: Short-Term Learning." *Animal Behavior* 33 (1985): 927–39.

———. "Evidence for Search Image in Blackbirds, *Turdus merula* L.: Long-Term Learning." *Animal Behavior* 33 (1985): 1301–09.

Lawrie, W. H. *Scottish Trout Flies.* London: Frederick Muller, 1966.

Leopold, Aldo. *A Sand County Almanac.* New York: Oxford University Press, 1949.

Magee, Leslie. *Fly Fishing: The North Country Tradition.* Otley, West Yorkshire: Smith and Settle, 1994.

Marinaro, Vincent. *In the Ring of the Rise.* New York: Crown, 1976.

———. *A Modern Dry-Fly Code.* New York: Putnams, 1950.

Martin, Darrel. *The Fly Fisher's Illustrated Dictionary.* New York: Lyons Press, 2000.

McClane, A. J. *The Practical Fly Fisherman.* New York: Prentice-Hall, 1953.

McDonald, John. *Quill Gordon.* New York: Knopf, 1972.

Montgomery, Monty. *The Way of the Trout.* New York: Knopf, 1991.

Mottram, J. C. *Fly Fishing: Some New Arts and Mysteries.* London: The Field & Queen (Horace Cox), 1915.

Murray, William Henry Harrison. *Adventures in the Wilderness.* Boston: Ticknor & Fields, 1869.

Nemes, Sylvester. *The Soft-Hackled Fly.* Old Greenwich, CT: Chatham Press, 1975.

———. *Two Centuries of Solf-Hackled Flies.* Mechanicsburg, PA: Stackpole Books, 2004.

Norris, Thaddeus. *The American Angler's Book.* Philadelphia: E. H. Butler, 1864.

Overfield, T. Donald. *G. E. M. Skues: The Way of a Man with a Trout.* London: Ernest Benn Limited, 1977.

Pritt, Thomas Evan. *Yorkshire Trout Flies.* London: Sampson Low, Marston, Searle & Rivington, 1885. Republished 1886 as *North-Country Flies.*

Proper, Datus. *What the Trout Said.* New York: Knopf, 1982.

Radcliffe, William. *Fishing from the Earliest Times.* London: Murray, 1921.

Reid, Pamela J., and Sara J. Shettleworth. "Detection of Cryptic Prey: Search Image or Search Rate?" *Journal of Experimental Psychology: Animal Behavior Processes* 18, no. 3 (July 1992): 273.

Rhead, Louis. *American Trout Stream Insects.* New York: Frederick Stokes, 1916.

Ringler, Neil. "Individual and Temporal Variation in Prey Switching by Brown Trout, *Salmon trutta.*" *Copeia* 4 (1985): 918–26.

———. "Selective Predation by Drift-Feeding Brown Trout *(Salmon trutta).*" *Journal of the Fisheries Research Board of Canada* 36 (1979): 392–403.

———. "Variation in Foraging Tactics of Fishes." In *Predators and Prey in Fishes,* edited by David L. G. Noakes, David G. Lindquist, Gene S. Helfman, and Jack A. Ward, 159–71. The Hague: Dr W. Junk Publishers, 1983.

Ringler, Neil and David F. Brodowski. "Functional Responses of Brown Trout (*Salmo trutta* L.) to Invertebrate Drift." *Journal of Freshwater Ecology* 2, no. 1 (March 1983): 45–57.

Rome, Lawrence C., Douglas Swank, and David Corda. "How Fish Power Swimming." *Science* 261 (July 16, 1993): 340–43.

Ronalds, Alfred. *The Fly-Fisher's Entomology.* London: Longman, 1836. Reprint, Secaucus, NJ: Wellfleet Press, 1990.

Samuel, William. *The Arte of Angling.* London: Henry Middleton, 1577. Reprinted as Appendix in Izaak Walton, *The Compleat Angler,* London: Oxford University Press, 1960.

Schullery, Paul. *American Fly Fishing: A History.* New York: Nick Lyons Books, 1987.

———. *The Bears of Yellowstone.* 3rd ed. Worland, WY: High Plains Publishing, 1992.

———. An Early Illustration of a Rising Trout. *American Fly Fisher* 16, no. 2 (1990): 10–11.

———. "The Fly-Fishing Stories in Winslow Homer's Art." In *Winslow Homer: Artist and Angler,* edited by Patricia Junker with Sarah Burns, 70–93. Amon Carter Museum, Fort Worth, Texas, and Fine Arts Museums of San Francisco/Thames and Hudson, London, 2002.

———. "How Trout Take a Fly." *Fly Fisherman* (May 2003): 42–45, 75–77.

———. *Mountain Time.* New York: Nick Lyons Books/Schocken, 1984.

———. "Predators and Prey at Fishing Bridge." *Yellowstone Science* (Spring 2003): 31–39.

———. "The Reel Woman: A Fish Story." *New York Times Book Review* (July 7, 1996): 19.

———. *Royal Coachman: The Lore and Legends of Fly Fishing.* New York: Simon & Schuster, 1999.

———. *Searching for Yellowstone.* New York: Houghton Mifflin, 1997.

Schwiebert, Ernest. *Trout.* New York: Dutton, 1978.

Scotcher, George. *The Fly Fisher's Legacy.* Chepstow, England: M. Willett, c. 1810–1819. Reprint, London: Honey Dun Press, 1974.

Scott, Genio. *Fishing in American Waters.* New York: Orange Judd Company, 1875.

Scott, Jock. *Greased Line Fishing for Salmon.* London: Seeley, Service, 1933. Reprint, Rockville Centre, NY: Freshet Press, 1970.

Scrope, William. *Days and Nights of Salmon Fishing in the Tweed.* London: Murray, 1843.

Sholseth, Thomas. *How Fish Work: Fish Biology and Angling.* Portland, OR: Frank Amato, 2003.

Skues, George E. M. *Minor Tactics of the Chalk Stream.* London: Black, 1910.

———. *Side-Lines, Side-Lights, and Reflections.* London: Seeley, Service, 1932.

———. *The Way of a Trout with a Fly.* London: Black, 1921.

Sosin, Mark, and John Clark, *Through the Fish's Eye: An Angler's Guide to Gamefish Behavior.* New York: Harper & Row, 1973.

Stewart, William. *The Practical Angler.* Edinburgh: Black, 1857.

Stolz, Judith, and Judith Schnell. *Trout.* Harrisburg, PA: Stackpole Books, 1991.

Swisher, Doug, and Carl Richards. *Emergers.* New York: Lyons Press, 1991.

———. *Selective Trout.* New York: Crown, 1971.

Taverner, Eric. *Divers Ways to Tackle Trout.* London: Chatto & Windus, 1925.

———. *Trout Fishing from All Angles.* London: Seeley, Service, 1929.

Tinbergen, L. "The Natural Control of Insects in Pinewoods. I. Factors Influencing the Intensity of Predation by Songbirds. *Archives Neerlandaises de Zoologie* 13 (1960): 265–343.

Tod, Ewen. *Wet-Fly Fishing Treated Methodically.* London: Sampson Low, Marston, 1903.

Traver, Robert. *Trout Madness*. New York: St. Martin's, 1960.

———. *Trout Magic*. New York: Crown, 1974.

Turton, John. *The Angler's Manual*. 1836.

van Leeuwen, J. L. "A Quantitative Study of Flow in Prey Capture by Rainbow Trout, *Salmo gairdneri*, with General Consideration of the Actinopterygian Feeding Mechanism," *Transactions of the Zoological Society of London* 37 (1984): 171–227.

van Leeuwen, J., and M. Muller. "Optimum Sucking Techniques for Predatory Fish." *Transactions of the Zoological Society of London* 37 (1984): 137–169.

Varley, John D., and Paul Schullery. *Freshwater Wilderness: Yellowstone Fishes and Their World*. Yellowstone National Park: Yellowstone Library and Museum Association, 1983. Revised, enlarged, and republished as *Yellowstone Fishes: Ecology, History, and Angling in the Park,* Mechanicsburg, PA: Stackpole Books, 1998.

Walton, Izaak. *The Compleat Angler*. Edited by Rev. George Washington Bethune. New York: Wiley & Putnam, 1847 [first Bethune edition of the Walton-Cotton 1676 edition, with Bethune's original essay on American fly fishing].

———. *The Compleat Angler*. London: John Lane, Bodley Head, 1897. Reprint, London: Senate, 1994.

Ward, Francis. *Animal Life under Water*. London: Cassell, 1919.

———. *Marvels of Fish Life*. London: Cassell, 1911.

Webster, David. *The Angler and the Loop-Rod*. Edinburgh: William Blackwood and Sons, 1885.

Weihs, D. "Hydrodynamics of Suction Feeding in Fish in Motion." *Journal of Fisheries Biology* 16 (1980): 425–33.

Wells, Henry Parkhurst. *Fly-Rods and Fly-Tackle*. New York: Harper Brothers, 1885.

Wheatley, Hewett. *The Rod and Line*. London: Longman, Brown, Green, & Longmans, 1849.

Whitlock, Dave. "Riseforms." *Trout* (Summer 2004): 56–58.

Willers, Bill. *Trout Biology: A Natural History of Trout and Salmon*. New York: Lyons & Burford, 1991.

Wilson, James. *The Rod and the Gun*. Edinburgh: Black, 1844.

Wotton, Roger S., and Terence M. Preston. "Surface Films: Areas of Water Bodies That Are Often Overlooked." *BioScience* 55, no. 2 (February 2005): 137–45.

Wright, Leonard. *Fishing the Dry Fly as a Living Insect*. New York: Dutton, 1972.

———. *The Ways of Trout*. New York: Nick Lyons Books, 1985.

Younger, John. *River Angling for Salmon and Trout*. Enlarged second edition, Kelso, England: Rutherfurd, 1864. Reprint edition, Devon, England: The Flyfisher's Classic Library, 1995.

ACKNOWLEDGMENTS

I thank my wife, Marsha Karle, not only for taking time from her water-colors to produce the drawings for this book, but also for her endless support and enthusiasm for my work and for sharing so many wonder-filled days along so many beautiful rivers.

Literary agent Rick Balkin, my friend and advisor for twenty years now, patiently and cheerfully guides me through each new project no matter how obscure the book's subject. It's always great to work with Judith Schnell, Amy Lerner, and the folks at Stackpole Books, whose sense of professionalism and enthusiasm for trout never fade.

About thirty years ago, fellow Yellowstone naturalist Chris Judson showed me a beautiful slide she'd taken of cutthroat trout at Fishing Bridge. That image inspired my long, patient intention of some day taking similar photographs and finally led me out on the bridge to start taking the pictures that resulted in this book.

And this reminds me that I am inexpressibly grateful to the cutthroat trout of the Yellowstone River in Yellowstone National Park. These fish have provided us with so much joy and beauty for so long, but we have rewarded them with the catastrophic introduction into their lovely world of non-native organisms that threaten their continued existence. This book is only one small testament to the immense good these fish have done us. We must save them and their world.

Good friends have made the world of fly fishing more enriching than I ever could have imagined when I started fishing more than thirty years ago. John Varley remains my foremost guide and advisor in the technical world of fisheries research and management. Bud Lilly's vast experience with trout and fishermen is always a source of enjoyment and wisdom. My brother Steve has constantly raised interesting thoughts and questions about fish and fishing. And Dale Greenley has proved that someone can be a world-class fishing pal even if you hardly ever actually get to fish together. It says a lot about fly fishing that all of these people have a great sense of humor. I've learned more than I can say from them, but it's the conversations and laughs I remember most.

Fellow historians of fly fishing John Betts, Ken Cameron, Andrew Herd, Richard Hoffmann, and David Ledlie have all been helpful, inspiring, and entertaining correspondents in this peculiar little field of interest. Trout science experts Robert Bachman, Robert Behnke, and Neil Ringler have been generous with publications, ideas, and responses to my theories and questions as I've explored the feeding behavior of trout and other subjects.

For many years, I've been a grateful visitor to Yellowstone National Park's superb library, museum collection, and archives and at times have even been in charge of some or all of this unique set of resources. As I finish this manuscript, the National Park Service has just opened its beautiful new Heritage and Research Center at Yellowstone's North Entrance, finally providing the park's extraordinary cultural and scientific treasures with a storage and research facility to match their significance to the world. The staff members of many of these collections have been unfailingly helpful over the years. Park historian Lee Whittlesey, my friend and frequent coauthor in other fields, has for many years kept a special lookout for unusual and obscure trout-related documents on my behalf.

Generations of dedicated managers have performed the immense public service of caring for Yellowstone's aquatic resources, protecting them for all of us against the onslaughts of politics, exotic invasions, and our own shortsightedness as anglers. The National Park Service needs our prolonged and forceful assistance to wage the battle that is currently under way against whirling disease, lake trout, and other dire problems facing Yellowstone's aquatic ecosystem. For more information on how you can help, contact the Superintendent, P.O. Box 168, Yellowstone Park, WY 82190.

Montana State University's wonderful Trout and Salmonid Collection has in recent years grown into a bibliographical treasure of international significance. Dean of libraries Bruce Morton, special collections librarian Kim Allen Scott, and numerous library staffers have been of great help in my research into fish, fishers, and their strange ways.

Because my book in good part continues a multicentury dialogue among fishing writers, I cite and quote dozens of earlier books and other publications. But I must single out the *American Fly Fisher,* the quarterly journal of the American Museum of Fly Fishing; its accumulated pages are nothing less than an encyclopedia of fly-fishing culture, lore, and technical history.

186

Others who have helped with advice, encouragement, or information include John Good, E. J. Malone, Tom Rosenbauer, Rev. Robert Spaight, Gary Tanner, and the many people who came up to me after my formal presentations of my photographs and asked interesting questions I couldn't answer.

A special thanks to Steve and Marilynn French, long-time grizzly bear researchers, for introducing me to the finer points and greater satisfactions of long-distance wildlife observation many years ago.

In this book, I have reprinted several illustrations of rising trout from Eric Taverner's *Trout Fishing from All Angles* (1929) and two illustrations from Fred Everett's *Fun with Trout* (1952). Though every effort has been made to determine the current ownership of the rights to these illustrations, in both cases the exact status of copyright remains unclear. Based on the strong likelihood that these works are no longer under copyright, and a concerted, good-faith effort to learn otherwise, I have felt comfortable using them here. If any reader has more information on these rights, I would appreciate hearing from him, care of the publisher, Stackpole Books, 5067 Ritter Road, Mechanicsburg, PA 17055.

The cheerful and skilled people at F11 Photographic Supplies in Bozeman, Montana, have taken excellent care of my film processing, scanning, and other photographic needs for many years. Sandra Nykerk helped me preserve many of the original trout images in this book by scanning them before I began to scatter them around the country to magazines and publishers.

Last, I am pleased to have made a start at considering many of these topics in magazine articles. Several magazines and journals have published much shorter versions of some chapters, as follows (in alphabetical order): *American Angler,* chapters 3, 6, 8, 10, 11, 12, and 13; the *American Fly Fisher,* chapter 9; *Fly Fisherman,* chapters 2 and 4; and *Yellowstone Science,* chapter 2 (a revised version of the *Fly Fisherman* article). My thanks to Phil Monahan at *American Angler,* Kathleen Achor at the *American Fly Fisher,* John Randolph and Jay Nichols at *Fly Fisherman,* and Alice Wondrak Biel and Roger Anderson at *Yellowstone Science* for their interest and help.

INDEX

Page numbers in italics indicate illustrations.

Aelian, 109, 110–12, 115, 116
American Angler's Guide
    (Brown), 164
American Fly Fishing (Schullery),
    152, 166
American Museum of Fly
    Fishing, 10
American Trout Stream Insects
    (Rhead), 48, 155
The Angler and the Little Fish
    engraving (Bewick), *90*
The Angler and the Loop-Rod
    (Webster), 91, 140, 172
Angler's Manual (Turton), 140
Animal Life Under Water
    (Ward), 41
The Art of Trout Fishing on Rapid
    Streams (Cutcliffe), 142
The Arte of Angling (Samuel), 1
The Astorga Manuscript
    (Bergara), 161

Bachman, Robert, 28, 58, 70–71
Bainbridge, George, 37, 89
Bartram, William, 166
The Bears of Yellowstone
    (Schullery), 7
Behnke, Robert, 96, 97

Beneath the Surface (Coston), 51
Benhart Creek, Montana, 128
Bergara, Juan de, 161–62
Bergman, Ray, 50, 55, 119, 155, 156
Bethune, George Washington, 175
Bewick, Thomas, engravings by,
    90, 115, 165
A Book on Angling (Francis), 153
Borger, Gary, 107
Braekman, Willy, 112
The British Angler's Manual
    (Hofland), 152, 164
Brook and River Trouting
    (Edmonds and Lee), 140
Brooks, Charles, 105, 166–67
Brooks, Joe, 119, 147
Brown, John, 164
bulging trout, *44*
Burke, Edgar, 156
Burks, Barnard, 61
Byrnes, Gordon, 81

Cameron, Ken, 36, 95, 155
Camp, Samuel, 48, 118
Canoeing in the Adirondacks
    watercolor (Homer), 33, *34*
Carrie Stevens (Hilyard and
    Hilyard), 156
Carroll, Dixie, 153
Casting, "A Rise" watercolor
    (Homer), 34, *35*

casting techniques
bobbing and swimming, 164–66
bouncing, 168–69
cross-lining, 172–73
dapping, 161–64, *165*
disturbing the mirror, 169–70
fluttering, 167–68
skating, 171–72
skipping, 171
slapping, 166–67
tick, 169
catch-and-release fishing, 82,
91, 99
Clark, John, 77
Clark Creek, Pennsylvania, *119*
Clarke, Brian, 41, 60, 79
interpreting riseforms, 54–55
Compleat Angler (Walton), 162
The Compleat Sportsman
(Jacob), 172
Connett III, Eugene, 61, 131
Coston, H. E. Towner, 50–51, 56
Cotton, Charles, 162, 163–64
Cress Spring Creek, Montana, *127*
Cutcliffe, H. C., on hackles, 142–43

Davy, Humphrey, Sir, 37–38, 162
*Days and Nights of Salmon Fishing
in the Tweed* (Scrope), 153
DeMott, Bob, *128*
Denham, engraving of, *162*
Divers Ways to Tackle Trout
(Taverner), 44
The Dry Fly (LaFontaine),
169, 171
The Dry Fly and Fast Water
(LaBranche), 48, 168
*Dry-Fly Fishing, Theory and
Practice* (Halford), 39, 118
Dunne, J. W., 129

Edmonds, Harfield, 140
Everett, Fred, 161

feeding, 18–19
expelling the fly, 71–73, *72*
hits, 70–71
misses, 66–69
rejection, *67, 69*
suction, 22–27, 65–66, *66*
takes, *73*, 73–75, *74*
feeding lane, 56
Firehole River, Yellowstone
Park, *111*
fish photography, 7–13
underwater, 40
Fisherman's Fall (Haig-Brown),
29, 178
Fishing in American Waters
(Scott), 150
Fishing Bridge, 4–7, *6*, 10–13, 59
waters beneath, *11*
*Fishing the Dry Fly as a Living
Insect* (Wright), 160
Fishing from the Earliest Times
(Radcliffe), 108
Fishing with Floating Flies
(Camp), 118
Fishing Tackle and Kits
(Carroll), 153
*Floating Flies and How to Dress
Them* (Halford), 39
The Fly (Herd), 113, 116, 117, 149
A Fly Dresser's Work Bench
painting (Wood), *154*
Fly Fisherman, 70, 81
Fly-Fisher's Entomology
(Ronalds), 37, 79, 89
Fly Fisher's Guide (Bainbridge),
37, 89
*The Fly Fisher's Illustrated
Dictionary* (Martin), 139
Fly Fisher's Legacy (Scotcher), 89
fly fishing
catch-and-release, 82, 91, 99
double-rod, 172
dry, 39

history of, 109–16
tradition, 105–8
upstream vs. downstream,
    118–21
see also casting techniques;
    fly patterns
Fly Fishing (Magee), 140
Fly Fishing (Mottram), 45
fly patterns, 94–95
    Beaconsfield, *152*
    beadhead, *122*, 122–23
    Bivisible, *134*
    bucktail, *135*
    Crimson Woodcock, 144
    Dabbler, *134*
    dry, *160, 177*
    Gray Ghost, 156, *158*
    Green Mantle, *151*
    Grizzly King, *151*, 156
    Light Spruce, *157*
    Long Tom, *151*
    Partridge and Orange, 144
    The Professor, *151*
    Renegade, *134*
    Royal Coachman, 155
    salmon, 154
    saltwater streamer, *135*
    Sam Slick, *151*
    Snipe and Purple, 144
    soft-hackled, *139, 141*
    spider, *141*
    streamer, *135*, 152–53
    wet, *134*, 149–50, *150, 151*
    Yellow Professor, 156
*The Flyfisher & the Trout's Point of
    View* (Harding), 45, 132, 144
Fly-Rods and Fly-Tackle (Wells), 156
Fogg, Roger, 140, 143, 144
Forest and Stream, 63, 64, 90
Francis, Francis, 70, 153, 154, 158
Freshwater Wilderness (Schullery
    and Varley), 9
Fun with Trout (Everett), 161

G. E. M. Skues (Overfield), 42
Gardner River, Montana, *9*
Garlick, Theodatus, 64
Gibbon River, Yellowstone
    National Park, *145*
Gierach, John, 122
Gill, Emlyn, 48, 50
Goddard, John, 41, 60, 79
    interpreting riseforms, 54–55
Good Flies (Gierach), 122
Gordon, Sid, 64, 73
Gordon, Theodore, 48
Greased Line Fishing for Salmon
    (Scott), 133
Green, Seth, 64
Green Spring Creek,
    Pennsylvania, *54*
Greenley, Dale, 125
Grove, Alvin "Bus," 107, 170
Grubb, Thomas, 77, 99, 170

Haig-Brown, Roderick L., 29,
    103, 178
Halford, Frederic, 48, 118, 121,
    123, 159, 176, 178
    analysis of the rise, 39–41
Hallock, Charles, 64
*A Handbook of North Country
    Trout Flies* (Fogg), 140, 144
Hanyok, Phil, *119*
Harding, E. W., 144
    analysis of the rise, 45–46
    hook experiments, 132–33
Herd, Andrew, 113, 114, 116, 117,
    132, 142, 145, 149, 172, 176
Herrero, Steve, 92
Hewitt, Edward, 134, 171
Hills, John Waller, 109–10, 112, 115
History of Fly Fishing for Trout
    (Hills), 109
Hoffmann, Richard, 112
Hofland, T. C., 152, 164
Homer, Winslow, 6, 33

hooks, 132
  Fly Body, *135*
  keel, *135*
How to Fish from Top to Bottom
  (Gordon), 64, 73
How Fish Work, Fish Biology and
  Angling, 77

In the Ring of the Rise (Marinaro),
  19, 51, 53, 71, 79, 88

Jackson, John, 140
Jacob, Giles, 172
Judy, John, 71, 120

Keene, John Harrington, 48
Kelson, George, 152
Koch, Ed, *98*
Kreh, Lefty, 105

LaBranche, George, 48–50, *49,*
  59, 161, 168–69
LaFontaine, Gary, 169–70, 171
Lawrie, W. H., 141
leaders, 125–26
Ledlie, David, *127*
Lee, Norman, 140
Leopold, Aldo, xi, xiii–xiv, 108
Letort Spring Run,
  Pennsylvania, *98*
Lilly, Bud, 94
Lure and Lore of Fly Fishing
  (Grove), 107, 170

McClane, A. J., 119
McClarn, Donald, 134
McDonald, John, 107, 109, 120, 123
McGuckin, Walter, 50
Magee, Leslie, 140
Malone, E. J., 151
Marinaro, Vincent, xii, 19, 21, 34,
  45–46, 59, 71, 79, 88, 95
  analysis of the rise, 51, 52–53

Marston, R. B., 48
Martin, Darrel, 139
Marvels of Fish Life (Ward), 41
The Mayflies, or Ephemeroptera,
  of Illinois (Burks), 61
The Mind of the Trout (Grubb), 77,
  99, 170
Minor Tactics of the Chalk Stream
  (Skues), 41
A Modern Dry-Fly Code
  (Marinaro), 51
Montgomery, Monty, 130
Moss, J. Edwards, 45
Mottram, J. C., 45
Mountain Time (Schullery), 7
My Friend the Trout (Connett III),
  61, 131

Nemes, Sylvester, 137, 138, 141
Nymphing (Borger), 107

observation pond, *40*
On the Characteristics of Animals
  (Schofield translation), 110
Orvis, Charles, 64
Overfield, T. Donald, 42
Oxford English Dictionary, 153

Parks, Richard, 75
postrise process, *57*
The Practical Angler (Stewart), 117,
  126, 140, 141
Practical Dry-Fly Fishing (Gill), 50
Practical Fly-Fisher (Jackson), 140
The Practical Fly Fisherman
  (McClane), 119
A Primer of Fly Fishing (Haig-
  Brown), 103
Pritt, Thomas Evan, 140
Proper, Datus, 107
pupfish, *9*

Quill Gordon (McDonald), 107, 120

Radcliffe, William, 108, 109
Rhead, Louis, 48, 155
Rhode, Homer, Jr., 135
Richards, Carl, 105, 106
Ringler, Neil, 18
riseforms, *37, 53*
  bulging, *44*
  conclusions concerning, 56–62
  correlation of speed with
    splashier, 60–61
  flash, 53
  head and tail, *46*
  kidney-shaped whorl, *43*, 44
  porpoise roll, *47*
  pyramid, *47*
  tailing, *45*
  waggle, 55
*River Angling for Salmon and
    Trout* (Younger), 153
The Rod and the Gun (Wilson),
    151, 152
The Rod and Line (Wheatley),
    63, 167
rods, 121–22
Ronalds, Alfred, 37, 79, 89
Rosenbauer, Tom, on brook trout,
    51–52
Royal Coachman (Schullery), 99

Salmon Fly (Kelson), 152
Salmonia (Davy), 38, 162
Salt Creek, Death Valley National
    Park, *9*
Samuel, William, 1
A Sand County Almanac
    (Leopold), xi
Sawyer, Frank, 52
Schnell, Judith, 77
Schofield, A. F., 110
Schullery, Dan, *107*
Schullery, Paul, *100, 145*
Schullery, Steve, *93, 107*
Schwiebert, Ernest, 47, 146

Scotcher, George, 89
Scott, Genio, 150
Scott, Jock, 133
Scottish Trout Flies (Lawrie), 141
Scrope, William, 153
Selective Trout (Richards and
    Swisher), 105, 106
Sholseth, Thomas, 77
*Side-Lines, Side-Lights, and
    Reflections* (Skues), 45, 91
Skues, George Edward Mackenzie,
    23, *42*, 43, 45, 91, 112–13,
    114, 121
  analysis of the rise, 41–45
  on visible hooks, 128, 129
Slack Line Strategies for Fly Fishing
    (Judy), 71, 120
Snell circle, 77–79, *78*
The Soft-Hackled Fly (Nemes), 137
Sosin, Mark, 77
Spaight, Robert, 61–62
Steamboat Creek, North Umpqua
    River, Oregon, *9*
Stevens, Carrie, 156–58
Stewart, William, 117, 126, 138,
    140, 141
Stolz, Judith, 77
strike detectors, 122
suction feeding, 22–27, 65–66, *66*
suction trough, 56
Sunrise, Fishing in the Adirondacks
    watercolor (Homer), 34, *35*
Sunshine and the Dry Fly
    (Dunne), 129
Swisher, Doug, 105, 106

tailing trout, *45*
Tanner, Gary, *111*, 146
Taverner, Eric, analysis of the rise,
    44–45, 46–47
three-fly rig, *161*
Through the Fish's Eye (Clark and
    Sosin), 77

Tinbergen, Niko, 130
Tod, Ewen, 89
Traver, Robert, 173, 175–78
Treatyse of Fishing with an Angle, 109
trout
  brook, 51–52
  brown, *9*, 91–94
  cutthroat, 16, *17–31*, 51, 92
  steelhead, *9*
Trout, 28, 53
Trout (Bergman), 50, 55, 119, 155, 156
Trout (Schnell and Stolz), 77
Trout (Schwiebert), 47, 53
Trout Biology (Willers), 73, 77
Trout Fishing (Brooks), 119, 147
Trout Fishing from All Angles (Taverner), 43, 44, 45, 46
The Trout and the Fly (Clarke and Goddard), 54
Trout Madness (Traver), 175
Trout Magic (Traver), 173
Trout and Salmon Fisherman for Seventy-Five Years (Hewitt), 171
Trout and Salmon of North America (Behnke), 96
The Trout and the Stream (Brooks), 166
Turton, John, 140

van Leeuwen, Johan, 20, 67
  on suction feeding in fish, 65–66
Van Siclen, George W., 63
Varley, John, 9
vision, field of, *80, 82, 83, 85*
  blind spots, 79–81
  dominant eye, 88

enlarging, *84*
flexible, 81–86
posture, 87–88
preferred angle, *86*, 86–87
window, 77–79

Walton, Izaak, 162, 164
Ward, Francis, 40, 41
Water Symphony (Coston), 51
Waterman, Charley, 95
The Way of the Trout (Montgomery), 130
The Way of a Trout with a Fly (Skues), 23, 43, 128
The Ways of Trout (Wright), 58
Webster, David, 91, 140, 172
Weihs, D., 25, 60, 61
Wells, Henry Parkhurst, 156
West-Fly Fishing Treated Methodically (Tod), 89
What the Trout Said (Proper), 107
Wheatley, Hewett, 63, 167–68
Whitlock, Dave, 70, 106
  analysis of the rise, 53–54
Willers, Bill, 73, 77
Wilson, James, 151, 152
window, 77–79, *78*
wings, scissoring, 147–48, *148*
Wood, Catherine M., painting by, *154*
Wood, Reuben, 64
Wright, Leonard, 58–59, 160–61, 171

Yellowstone Lake, 3
Yellowstone River, 3–4, *4, 5*
Yellowstone Science, 70
Yorkshire Trout Flies (Pritt), 140
Younger, John, 153